Collected Poems & Sequences
(1981-91)

Collected Poems & Sequences

(1981-91)

Bill Griffiths

Edited by Alan Halsey

REALITY STREET

Published by
REALITY STREET
63 All Saints Street, Hastings, East Sussex TN34 3BN
www.realitystreet.co.uk

First edition 2014
All rights remain with the estate of Bill Griffiths
Additional material copyright © Alan Halsey, 2014
Typesetting & book design by Ken Edwards
Cover image from a hand-coloured copy of *The Book of the Boat* in the collection of Allen Fisher

A catalogue record for this book is available from the British Library

ISBN: 978-1-874400-65-3

Preface

This volume is the successor to Bill Griffiths' *Collected Earlier Poems (1966-80)*, extending the account through the following decade. During the 1970s Griffiths had lived mainly in London, publishing much of his work through his own Pirate Press while also closely involved with Writers Forum and the Consortium of London Presses. The 1980s saw him move to Cowley, Middlesex, where he lived on a houseboat until its destruction in a welding-shop accident. There followed an itinerant period, spent partly on a caravan site at Brightlingsea, preceding his final move in 1990 to Seaham, County Durham. In the previous year he had founded a new imprint, Amra, initially publishing a backlog of poetry and prose. A distinct juncture appears in his work in 1991: once he had settled in Seaham the history, dialect and ethos of the north-east became his main focus. Griffiths was above all a poet alert to, inquisitive about and absorbed in his surroundings; in the later 1980s those had principally been his boat, the London waterways and the Thames estuary.

The earlier phase of his poetry was remarkable for the sheer quantity of work mostly published in short-run pamphlets which permitted frequent revisions and re-sequencing. The period 1981-86 shows a stark contrast: just three collections of new poems and relatively few magazine appearances. Most of the poems collected here were first published, and probably written, in the prolific years 1987-91 and practically all published by Writers Forum and Amra in very small editions. Many have not previously been reprinted and since this includes all the longer sequences, at least in intact form, there has been no widely available overview of the extraordinary compass of Griffiths' work in this decade.

The largely chronological order of poems in the collection for 1966-80 offered the soundest editorial approach to the textual mutability, interrelations and cross-reference of the 1970s pamphlets. A similar order was also an option for 1981-91, founded on the 'collected poems' which Griffiths assembled on digital files in 1991 and expanded in 1996. But since this would have dispersed the careful, coherent and self-contained gatherings evident in the pamphlets of this period it has seemed a preferable chronology to present the work as it appeared in those successive publications. Exceptions have been made to avoid repetition – *Quire Book*, for example, is reprinted here in its later appearance as Part 1 of *A Book of Legends*. In comparison with the earlier poems this 1980s work is textually stable although migrations and variations of passages persist, most notably in *The Book of the Boat*, *Morning Lands* and *Quire Book/A Book of Legends*, sequences sufficiently interrelated to need considering en bloc. Sections and excerpts from these and other longer poems were republished in revised versions, sometimes newly titled and without reference to their previous incarnations, in retrospective collections such as *Future Exiles* and *The Mud Fort*. Most appear here in their original form but readers will need to refer to the end-notes for significant variants and exceptions. The Amra miscellanies *North Scenes* and *Joanne's Book* (1992 and 1993) are included since they are entirely retrospective. A few poems dateable to 1991 but re-sequenced in later pamphlets have been held over for future collection.

Thanks again to Joanne Harman for her permission to publish this book. Thanks also to everybody whose enthusiasm for Bill Griffiths' poetry has been a constant encouragement and especially those who have given crucial advice and textual help: Fred Beake, Steve Clews, Marc Vaulbert de Chantilly, Ken Edwards, Allen Fisher, Harry Gilonis, Michael Mann, Chris McCabe, Robert Sheppard and Richard Tabor.

Alan Halsey
Nether Edge, January 2013

Contents

Further Songs & Dances of Death

... he had indeed planned four other numbers: the death of a monk, a gloomy fanatic who dies in his cell to the sound of a bell tolling in the distance, the death of a political exile, returning home, who is drowned within sight of his native land, the death of a young woman remembering her love and her last ball, and 'The Warrior Anika and Death'.

Calvocoressi's *Mussorgsky*

First Set

1. *The Hermit*

1 says it woz kid-murder   2 says OK I know it   1 says I was a kid nearly, not that bad of it, just years till it came round   2 says you know what happens   1 says you don't scare me, it's good   2 says who's gonna worry   1 said on a lectric line zip zip   2 says calm now   1 says what happened?   2 says that was a fit, down on the floor   1 says it's OK now, needa lie up OK   2 says I'll list you then   1 says just up   2 says look at my bones over your heart   1 says you're pretty white   2 says go and die now

2. *Anika*

… thundering, hunting – death on major wings – a red-blue skin – focus I in – on some love to my tally to a death-meeting – or drive off her brothers tugging their legs – no one like Death had a fighter live as me ever – two years for one, one for ten, I want – cows or cubs won't be worth that – you die, well I don't have to – my back iz as busy aza spoke – working it out

3. *The River*

… is like grey like grey – line bluish blackish – on a wet board, oughta warm – O old wire, rusty stands – is dip-green, the air is yella – land looks to – and an arm-round of chicklets smoky and dirty and some white – singing bold like barges and tugs, as big as my eye – int'rupting land – all other lumps drifting and water gone blue – air is pale – land-line-iz-water-line – hold long to hold – every bit rocks this head – thick or flameless – some sea-fish is there porting one round stone by mouth – non-stop a whole gang like that, just lazy – figures of the mud on late-drift, little slap of nape – get up now – look at the long long line

4. *The Dance*

Ahoy! spiders – come and dance around the hammer – mushrooms, get up and run! – sand be abashed before the law – the young are pure and light – their thoughts are uncrossed – the old are deceitful – and sneer at life – I will dance with his dark hair and his teeth – till the cakes taste dust – his long feet tap in the dance – how the hairs are brittle

Second Set

1. *Cave Cure*

chal-
ked cave
What a great scene – crevasse
flick here, there
the stunt viaduct enz
a loop iz the stomach
the flower
a smoke
c'lyx-studded, a roll a roll a roll

wait,
what passed
it was
now the four ties are in place like a gong
wait

more I run
what an air
this a laugh
public
an' survive

2. *The Warrior*

Do I want?
Oh, a coffee, please.
The warrior makes sanctuary
He is safe.
The warrior is inside a church.
Would you like a lift?
No thanx, I am walking.
I like look in the shopwindows after shutting,
    imagining buying things.
Outside now is the plague monster

It is terribly golden
It is actually a deadly view.
Snow! Snow!
I want to play please.
It is so quiet you can peer out and see, it's all clear.
Instead, thru the hole of the key-way
The golden beast
standing, moving, remoulding,
Orbits of flaming hair
genitals or vulva
changing and modular
Flowing, it is all gold, aweful and slender and golden, yes.
The death of Anika, so,
A warrior
Is attributed to this
Even tho he locked himself in.

3. *River Cure*

I am white as flour-paste (skin, limbs)
Then aglow amber, seaweed scented as I heal.
Sickanwhole, sickanwhole I build me like a coral
... chest ... flat flesh

tall, pale
leafy a eucalyptus place
top perch
upon mazy or misty river-way

tussles of rope
cow-pats
smiling parties pass seaward

So I am seeking
gentlish herbs
to right
my sinning self

Kaolin and oranges

feelinglessness ...
into the blue go
buildings and fog
what do I/you care about ...
there are baked-egg and sandy-coloured banks
nerve and lip, toe and nipple
all clothing over emotions of a Hindu mountain, black by vegetation

body shocks
jolts of blue and

out of the rain
pretty young parrots sing and play

4. *Dance Hymn*

T on the sword
look look
Nam sicut
somewhere at the eastern base.

mors in Adam data est
did these danceprints disappear
kill-keen close
your mouths are full of death

Till the coming of the fire
towers of pumice, caves of ash
'we have built more such prisons'
grizzly, simple patterns, everywhere

The mark of a T
the claw of the law
skippitting in the dust
T on ash-pots.

Materia Boethiana

Scenario

Theodoric, as leader of the Vizigoths,
had captured all Italy, even Rome itself ...

Alfred's Metre

... Then   was
a certain   NOBLE
in the city   of ROME
ELEVATED   to the CONSULSHIP,
a man dear   to his LORD
while   the GREEKS
still controlled   the main CITY.
He   was
an ADMIRABLE   MAN –
there had not been   among
the ROMANS   a BETTER
TREASURE-sharer   FOR
many a day.   He
was   WISE
above   almost ANYONE,
keen   for REAL honours,
a MAN   clever
in BOOK-learning.   BOETHIUS
the HERO   was CALLED
who   received
that   PROMOTION.
In   his
MIND   at all
TIMES   was
the WRONG   and
CONTEMPT   that
FOREIGN   KINGS
showed   them.
He was   loyal
to   the GREEKS,
conscious   of the
GLORIES   and
OLDEN rights   that

his ANCESTORS
so long POSSESSED
for themselves,
such GRACE and FAVOUR.
Then began he
CAREFULLY SERIOUSLY
to CONSIDER how
he could
THITHER DRAW
the GREEKS that
the CÆSAR
once more should
HAVE POWER
over his own.
He sent a MESSAGE
SECRETLY to the FORMER masters
and in GOD'S name
bade them keep
the ANCIENT alliances,
to COME again
to the CITY
that the councillors of the GREEKS
should DIRECT the ROMANS
and hold POWER as their RIGHT
was. When
THEODORIC the Amuling
learned of this
PLAN, he seized
that THANE
and had his OFFICERS
CLOSELY GUARD
the HERO. For he
was UNEASY
at heart, and had much FEAR
of the
EARL. He
had him BARRED up
inside the PRISON.
Then BOETHIUS
was GREATLY

troubled   in his MIND.
For long   he had ENJOYED
SUCCESS   under
the SKIES,   so
the worse   could
he   BEAR
MISFORTUNE   now that
it had   so
GRIMLY   arrived.
In DESPAIR   was
the MAN,   he could EXPECT
no MERCY,   he foresaw
no HELP   in that CONFINEMENT
but   he
lay   FLAT,
FELL   down prone
on   the
floor,   spoke
MANY   a word,
bitterly   DESPAIRED …

Karl Schmidt's Boethius Version

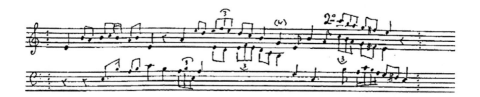

Boethius sitzt im Kerker eingeschlossen. Seine Bedrängnis
ist gross, da er keinen Trost finden kann. Verzweifelt
wirft er sich auf den Boden u. fasst weinend sein Leid in
Verse. (Boethius laments his fate)

Die Philosophie erscheint im Kerker, um ihren unglück-
lichen Schüler su trösten. (Philosophy enters his cell
to revive him)

"Hoffnung u. Schmerz sind nichts. Opes und honores sind
in Munde des Gesceadwisnes." (True rewards she sez are
the prerogative of Reason)

"Gesceadwisnes wie der Adler über die Wolken erhebt"
(Reason ascends like an eagle, she sez)

"That is scarcely appropriate, sighs Boethius. Their
intentions are clearly to punish me here, then con-
sign me to Hell!"

Link One

It was not yet
but it's not yet
near

a woman came out
whether he would go
a postcard there

the parapet
look at the new chimney
look at those
their neat house

and that game
here
a play of bottles
that snags and changes

Charm or Chant

(for Stuart Blackstock)

Lo the loud the
let the
over the dead, riding ...
loud they were, yes, loud,
Screya! loud in the rooms
such sound
sound mine.
One-minded, them,
sole-thoughted liars
who rode me thru my land.
So shield me you
Screya!
Shields you are

Christ!
yes, sound-stoppers sound-starters
what me?
Out, go,
out
spear-shout
shooter, calm, settle it,
land,
if you're in here
what, look the,
loud,
look,
dead-hill, out
beat
off
what loud they were.
I stood under a shield
light
bright, how!
that,
set-haired liars,
half-headers,
when the strong strangers
told over what was doing
(reach throw wade row)
done
are you shields then?
the mighty wife
making
street-sound,
tell over,
liar liar liar
what you do, you.
here
head, look, head,
Screya!
Yelling, yelling
let the, make the,
spear-speed
and they

shouting they sent
where
where sound
I
them
other one
back again
gotto, will
sound / send
loud
speeding spear
screya!
or face
or front
throat
stair
wall
stock
parapet
long live the
let
stand under linden
lope along
hoo-riders help
very light ones
loud they were
out
spear-part
if
they are
you are here still
again
spear-ones. scram.
sat the smith
struck
struck out
sword or sax
sound-maker!
screya!
little loud rooms

what! wounds those?
iron them?
head hold
have my shield
whole hall
hæftling loud
louder be
la
look
screamers
screws
screya!
what for
what wounds
what
iron
loud the
out
shout
spear if you're in
six smiths sitting
planning on
thing
they made
spears for slaying
work that
out spear!
not in not in
no
in sound in
it if
not any iron
steel-surround
work of witch
whole yellow
you
melt-you
must melt
it if was
hide-graze or heart-kick

vein-way
life-spinner
life-spiller
screya!
so you never
so there never be
shout
sound
shout
sound
sound-shouting
lo look loud lo.
against with
lords or laws
against the witch-one
this *shield*
for *sound.* Yo!
Can you climb
at all?
Ban then to
mountain-tip,
stay whole,
hale be
and who hears you.
Soft-speakers
down
are
as yoyos.
Or faced,
fought,
as no slow stomach,
none shallow shoulder,
land-shouter.   /
     / yo! /
      /

Link Two

The slow churning of earth
a global world
with strange sounds of chords
to the horizon.
The haze
and the hot and still
day
closes the head
of each of all,
the surface shine of the eye,
that we're
steelers and runners.
Like monarchs,
the giants set and guard.

Guide to the Giants of England

no (m)a(t)
-ter ov obsvn

a world which-in
grass ne grows
n'trees move, winds blow, milk soothes

lighter-darker summer-winter
brick with brick

along

up

no one
sees jiants

photo
fig. 000
      shows brix
not built with

banks of acres of rectangles
5 or 6 fields of new brix
put to dry

like letters in a bag

pausing

a record
where leaves don't imprint

fingers
only flat bones
and then luck

positive

in the smolt land
cleft and dale, dune, mount, nothing like,

or close to

no giant
would want
you to tell, that!

a gross patter-
rhythm track
to

grave woods
black with water
sharp, shivery and noisy

rent noses
of Yule, games, glamour

In self-index:
Habitat,
Observation,
Reverie,
Giants,
a sad Romance or interlude
and in conclusion, further giants then.

*

not fast
70 mph maybe about their maximum

                                                an

imagination in setting

ready enough
to call yourself a liar
to make a special study

                    or
their love of singing in wild weather
singing on the roof of Iona
in many cities
ripening grain
corn, engines, many another

there
by means of coloured rings
food-sources
Kale and root crops
                    maybe
adapted
helped to hang on
disappeared

these lists give us
total counts
week-ends, half-holidays
chief cause
            How/when
by means of
for me
two bits of ivory
one with a toothed edge

living
criss-crossing
is more of
tolerably regular
archaic
anywhere near you
seen at sea
            informed
Archaeopteryx
towards the end of the 19th century

means missing
worth making
            iris

the human shape

brecks newest
recent
number
rare and flourishing
'unspecialised' 'equal' 'good'
                                    was
in the war
a high-pitched 'chizzick'
summits of
gears or gorse

visit
vor wanne snow lith thicke and wide
an alle wihtes are close and spiteful
                                        attend, such
more hints
of rebuilding

there is still the chance
for
any young Londoner
to
make a name
by
a career of conquest
unequalled by any other
make good
good subjects

*

I pass the lines of dusk-buses
there are fires scenting the air

'One clear morn
is boon enuf for being born
and so it is'
says one lady or leader

in 1978, jiants were placed against some
'currently fashionable
egalitarian ethic' – but look!
it is not my recollection of the time

for
if the screaming don't abate by midnight
Christians will come and break
down ribs, diaphragms

It is this a pair of
jiant mirrors
set facing, reverberating
nothing new comes in, nothing can be seen but what's already sited,
reflected to myriads of misinforming
images or miracles – is that what is meant?

Try the source –
Do not be kidded
there is not much-any of honesty in your make-up
or would I want to be trusted?

thrust your face thru
the ice into the water
see the jiants are
great are the built courts of stone, the fish, the lion, their tramways

Empty! Crowded!
an ear-zeta wound with sound

over the creamy stones
of fresh graves
black now
th'air is pushed with sound
w'shingle, w'sad or discarded toys
not far from panic ...

*

Like a parade:

Gigantes autem erant   *Gen.6.4*
super terram in diebus illis
– jiants upon the earth

In
when a giant was disturbed ina cornfield
it presaged thunder and flooding:
History & Antiq. of Allerdale

In Geoffrey of Monmouth   *cf. Polyolbion xxi*
the Trojan Corineus wrestles Gogmagog at
Plymouth; too, such
were wood
and guarded London Bridge.
Fili hominis, pone faciem tuam   *Ezek.38.2*
contra Gog, terram Magog.
Son of man, set your face
against Gog, against the land of Magog.

At the end of the world
Satan was to be loosed after his 1000 years
et seducet gentes   *Revel.20.7-8*
quæ sunt super quattuor angulas terræ,
Gog et Magog,
and will lead these hosts of
Gog to battle.

How Bevis went in crusade
'and that (Goliath-like) great Ascupart enforc'd
to serve him for a slave, and by his hoss to run'
                                          Polyolbion ii

Ecce gigantes gemunt sub aquis
et qui habitant cum eis   *Job 26.5*
'The jiants shudder under the waters:
and the inhabitants thereof tremble'
they are
this is 'a legend analogous to that of Lake Asphaltites,

where the giants who had revolted against God
were submerged in the waters'   *Renan on Job*

These
and the 'Chorea Gigantum'
and the giant figures
and what more
all come to Christian mention
and shape
all come
from Christian mind, mode

puppets and
what they thought
pagans
thought like

*

Reviewing
the evidence
the jury will look a bit confused.

Do they need to think
of what happens next?

How Wade built Pickering and Mulgrave,
Gorm shaped the Avon Valley,
Hickathrift and Shonks, Ordulph,
Cormoran and Cormelian
did thus or thus, good or dead

How the pigs are
marched to be eaten
telling out jokes about teats

Listen you
that is the wicked
chuckling of Jack
in the settled air

smoke-cold before the time of evensong

It will be a coarse and brutal killing
that's something at any rate
mid rows of rungs
or a ring of earth-grins

with a long earth sigh
die

all blue, all red
knight krazy among the buffalo horns
sez trustier than zeal
honester than faith, showering down
peaches and all such-shaded fruits like
pineapple, tangerine. He is
Parkman surrounded with
injuns thieving, stabbing, slyly.

a fill up with grids of laws out of rights
now colder than a corner of stone
like 'heart the keener, 'solve bolder'
festivity, laughing and thieving I was thinking of

now come
that the giants stir
their stone stretches
from room to room
from door to door to floor

but the dancing's turned
to attrite giants
to pebbles and
the coupling
is to keep the figures
stone, still, out of world.

*

Would the jiants die if Brutus

unfounded Britain?

We could go to the boats of the orchard
and sleep there

the breccias of the beach
the slitting   flint
flake   and grate
and slip   on our soles
with sea-herb scent.

But a church sustaining its own giants
surly things
that turn milk and spoil intercourse,
break up touch
line up wall and door

these, giants: palaces
of lock and wall, so much of
talk, trust, reliance,
perimeters, trainees, maturement ...

And the stone
grows to all.
no waterfall of bulging wheat,
no paradise of sea-steam, of rain
not nothing to speak of, or no movement

But sacraments
new-made
of spike and thread and blob of amethyst,

loop and pyramid,

point and pump, call canal or free heart-way

carefully the rituals of shaking and mending

give away

get

part

begin

let/look

Jack of Legs
is buried in Weston Churchyard
near Baldock

Shonk
is buried beneath a wall
at Brent Pelham

Alfred's Prose

How can't you see   When the coils and chills unround
That each wort and each word   And each hare & each river
Will to wax   To save and extend
In the land   Of the air that is
Best that best suits   The burnt sun
Natural and comfortable   To the building and growing
There where it feels   By leaf and cheek
That it can quickest grow   Up in assist this moving & might
And most slowly fail   When the grave solar boats make by?
Some worts' or some woods'   Or demons, their
Place is on dunes   Or cliffs that face South,
Some amid marshes   In cities
Some on moors   Of pass-ways
Some on rocks   And frocks
Some on bare sands   That are day-singers.
Wherefore
Each seed creeps   From the blasts of night
Inside the earth   In its joy
And develops into   The forms of gems of
Sprouts and roots   Like coal & like bright orange pins
For no reason other than   Their power
To organise the stem   That is a sun-prop
And the helm   That is a moon-guard
Faster & taller reaching   Than the eggs of a science.
So from the roots   The notes blow
Upwards by the stem   And
Along its tunnels
And along the bark-ways   That are corks & siphons of
(to) The helm   Where it is a harmony
And then the boughs   That cut the black
So it spreads as   Universally as
Leaves & flowers   That print on the Sunny eye
And fruit   Ready on the blankest day.

November

Migne's printing
of Bede's *Mensium Notæ*
has a November wood-cut:
a bumpy field is shin-deep with snow
a short-cloaked traveller is caught in the open
between two solid-ink dogs.
He has his spear at the jaw of one
while the other attacks him from
behind and his hat has already tumbled off.
Near the row of trees in the background
someone is walking along with a stick
and someone is creeping up on him with a cudgel.

Thus,
caught between the Ice and the Ice Maiden.

danger,
continual, irremedial anger
in the creeks and viks of the stars
in the cool-way day-time

sky-scratches, day-swings
it is an open harvest of foundlings and demons

late and vast spiders yet spun
stained glass
over
and over and in the arcades
waterhorses slip and jeer with day-fulls of complaints

equally the filth of beetles
and the cochineal in the chalice,
matches of lions
and air-circles of dragons, the pomp of it!

we have killed
or badly injured a multitude of plants

(says Darwin)

it is autumn certainly
little presses are pegged up to dry to be packed away.

do your feet meet?
are your ears near?
do your eyes di-verge?
are your soles whole?
oh do your fingers sing?

I am storing fifty-one seeds of Goatsbeard:
so I can sow again.
Now I have lost them. Now I search again.

The Hawksmoor Mausoleum

1
Can cities have health?
and, are they surer places?
Bridges –
where? and for who?
silent, empty, in sequence.

2
A great rotunda
of balancing,
of balanced drums
(performances).
curved
ribbed
as the horn of a ram
almost part of the land.

3
Ravenna, certainly,
is evoked,
and
Theodoric,
the stones
drawn ready around.
Who lives in this shiny circling house?
Why, it is empty!
A hollow, resonant
Land I walk on.

4
Through the fibres of the park
I took this snow-way and that.
My breath whited and greyed, varied.
Petrified,
defensive,
intensely smokey,
it is as a balancer of fog –

cold air / cold sea
so the jewel, the crown
dissolve

5
Pages as
better records as regards
the hides of goats
than lime
or brown tile?
Or will any of it?
Such at
the leap
ova calf.

6
This one
speaks of the same time-tumble too.
Others
stars suns storms.
A torrential land
like glasses tuned and sharded.

7
Consider the landscape.
and the way of construction of them.
Probably
the daughter of the cuckoo king
– the niece of the invisible ones –
chose it so.
Now
because it is fearful
the land.

8
The stone rhymes
limps
reads.
But a breeze
– the season is such –

the sea keeps turning and turning upon itself
itiz a sort of drying drum.

9
But making
pure sound?
Imagine
          continuing as sound!

10
So high
in the house
only the birds' wings' sounds ...

11
The strange site
sight of circular rails.
Here
there
a little cretin of a Christian
or a land-holder
a dance he is forming out.

12
'Fraid, scaring humans
excavated
from a million cells
or sheds. How ill we are held.

13
Now, because it is fearful,
the Land.
With farts and churned feet
Six gaunt-hipped cattle fill
the grey field,
forked and clear spiteful.

14
The throb
of great

water-beasts
travels
the fair.

15
Adios
sez the
sun boat structure
before the blue rock.

16
The county is a gross shell,
you walk on it
you bounce you bowl on it
like a gigantic burp
and the Passage
is un-
jovial.

17
Transit

18
Look again
at the land
how parentless
complex complete grown and ordinary.

19
In the zone of confinement
the boy fighter
the glass jar
and the djinn.
in that stark and surly round of a place
the body is dumb
the teeth
move in the mouth.

20
Now now
I will balance you, out
just on the
shelves of my shoulders.

Eight Barques for the Manifold Soul of G.L. Renfree

1. The material or *Khat*

ah! before the weights
the air wraps or clogs
on the frame, is second
balance, thrust, care
what blocks the shoulders
last, over, lifting ground to
setting the muscles
in its habits
here the chest will arch
the spine rise nearly, it is
thus, the aspect, the *Khat*

'torted
lamellibranch
the case is light
like a spiral

this is the *Sahu* (the body, left)
pinned
or placed
as no Christian object walks
but Nut, the sky, the whole starry sky
lies in the lid
(and is sufficient retention)

2. The Canopic Jars

The glories,
the shred of lint that one saint
had banners of
now boxed

Great bars
and works

mixed up as a salad.
This is the band of the head,
Impresses of meaning
once them walking and cycling
under the sun,
special and peaceful.

These are the Colours
the tapes of thought
not intending to stay.

3. The *Ab* or Heart

As soft
brown light
informing or feeding
feeling

The image is
True arrows
shot in proper line
and time.

4. The *Ka* or terrestrial soul
(The separated one, the home seeker,
the stroller or silent visitor, the buzz of continuation,
the imperfect base of misaligned judger)

We wakened to sheer dark –
'get up! – get up!' – or blue?
It can't be time yet.
Where's the drink?
Kuzka – the drink!   OVER THE RIVERS.
                         IN THE QUARTERS.
                         THE SUN IS BUSY
                         WAKING EVERYONE.
shto! shto! where's our trousers?
shto! shto! where are our mausers?

now! now! who shall lead us?
nay! nay! you're
bound to lose us!

ON THE
BANK OF THE MORNING
BETWEEN THE HOUSE
AND THE TREE.
SAT A COLOSSAL GUARDSMAN
KEEPING WATCH
VERY NARROW-

shto! shto!   LY
where are the finders?
shto! shto! where are the winders?
nay! nay! who are the senders?
nay! nay! you are
but enders!

IN THE
HEART OF THE HOUSE.
SAT THERE THE GIRL
OF QUIET HAND.
SHE WOULD EVADE NOW
HER WATCHER
AND FIND HER WAY
ACROSS THE

Le'ss play   LAND.
at whiskey-miners!
Le'ss play at organ-grinders!
Le'ss play at engine-minders!
See if the fools can
bind us!

SETTING
HIS LEFT FOOT FAST FORWARD
CAME THE GUARD.
TO SEAL THE PATH.
BUT AS HE FLUNG FAR HIS BOTTLE
HE CRASHED
AND LAY ASLEEP IN THE HEARTH.

5. The Vital power or *Sekhem*

What stops
laughed, stupid, true, do

What is lost
the cheap train
the air: yellows and reds, unknown flower heads

What was the essential of all
Fast colours, the city,
its orange tree just in fruit, a salt taste, the boasting, slow, yellow

What was the energy that is never kept
This one, a clear, cold, sun-hoarding sea, the spreading
peacock heights, dead

What races back to the sun
down, and the air around, empty of angels

6.

The essence
The *Khu*
'it seems to have been
a shining, translucent, transparent, intangible essence.'

It isn't passed
from father to friend from daughter to duck
but finds, locates, accepts for itself,
Renders
Kingship, estate, inheritance a nothing
(As tho it was word or music everywhere!)

7. The *Ba* or hawk-formed soul,
that journeys to paradise

escaping the Nine Worms in the wastes	SO
propitiating the great serpent Aapep in his ambush	THE
to elude the Great Crocodile	SONG
two Serpents	OR
the Lynx	SPELL
the Beetle	IS

the Snake-Goddess	PLAYED
and others that feed on the transit of souls.	IN
Thus to the Henu-boat of Seker the Death-God.	TRAVEL
to the judgement of Osiris	AS
part riddle part interrogation,	THO
who can make you	THE
Golden Hawk	RATTLE
Being of Light	OF
Benu Bud	MILK-TOPS
Heron, Lily and Swallow.	IS
The provision	ANY
is a ladder	HELP
on which to climb into heaven.	HERE

8.

The *Khaibit* –
What is it?
Like an insect
In the soft, clicking air
as some night-flares come and pass
all uncertainly.
Or it howls silently
finding no place a'desert
The Khaibit Shadow
seeking out the Ba.

Link Three

In these closed systems, there are
Giant enterprises, and informations,
set to make themselves continue.
Or you can set against it too
what can always be born,
maybe that is usefuller to us
than what simply continues?
But Boethius
can use only the most past of shadows
to re-form his shattered place,
where all times gather into one,
an otherworld
that shamans, poets, philosophers
see into and cheat us with,
as tho any information will do.
'But them, people, they don't care what's happening'
    sez Eric.
'But look at what they're encouraged to look at,
    see the diversion' I say. Or I say
'Why don't people go, look, find for themselves?'
'They haven't the resources' sez Eric.
And still there is reckonably anything all possible
If you would feel like living in the open.

The Peacock Variations

1. (Theme)
invisibly
mistfully
sightfullessly
waking
all around sat the raw works of nature
shifting an' preenin'
pulling the snow out their ears.
There is much business today.

2. tread
step
pace
loping now
these are empty ways, transits
settled or painted

3. bang
bustle, here as gentle
aim
the wings of many people
knock and shake together
in the smack of new sense

4. faster
is louder / go

5. the slow slope of work
pads and pats
at the time,
whose tune never wipes / wipes clear

6. surges
lightens
looks
at the first spread
of light-givers

like sky-matches

7. stand
gently
tho there is no link
they simply equal
one thing another thing too,
tho the fade takes or mutes
that

8. this is
sheer, sure
chord of way-making
a crowd of saying.

9. how it runs, for a bit of time,
to goodwill even (and loving)
that is a multitude of movement

10. flutes
the shadows of the wing-pens
on wall
or door
that is for breathing
these are even
and start to talk, and can

11. sharp
alert
is the making and action (intent)
of many
run here, soft on foot

12. the slower
pulse of
not high not ranging
but of reeds
weaving comfort
with each rolling stitch. too,
is an acid tempo

now,
or stops.

13. the dredgers
move across the building
is their anger
something of the bright bird
to be matched
and flamed again
several
and single

14. the whole
the total
not grasped to ever be
is here
as sure as the soul of the winger
passes from back to back.

15. let the slow certainty
be padded or drummed
about
in the gentle waft of air
that means
the great flight of its wings
near
or not to be touched.

16. emerges
then out brick or iron, now as ghost-passer,
as a clear trill
of note, new,
as wide or high
as the ground-see-ers
never expected for it.
It is also here, have
And it is there / like itself.
A share, and clarifact,
attained, all too, if never guessed
that.

17. Jaunt or stroke
of own light jubilee,
answer, of the thick pounding halls
of stay, still, stand, must salute even
the hint of when it's
something (so urgent (so near to

18. Whether
it is confident for this,
that derides the old weighing clash
of stale trance and place.

19. to blow
or stamp
on the dark wall
on the cell of pasted black

20. riding   to the unpinned
floor-sky   and the new pressure
of opened   weather,   shimmers and leaps

21. What if it passes too? I can tell it anyway, form and message, that
I see its spread or its foot-root or bill-slam
up.

The Bournemouth

I

A chain of littled circumstances
From my scored thumb
To the sugar-tub – This is the way
The line
Marks itself (para', s'tence)

Where when the dead visited Outremer
When the sun in the sea turned to brown
And blew like dust – how
Can we care with the living
Without first knowing the dead?

Based in the amber place of the soil,
And the living threads
Worked loose – sending out,
Sensing their damage
In the dark.

Where the riders sealed their heads,
Dead, bled,
This company – with hawsers for hands
And spoke like locks,
Thrashing and calling their way.

To the worship of the Lady Lark:
The tap, the panes of light,
The pristine and sativate – smeared
With globes of in-colour,
Bobs and pig'radiance.

Debtors, who when their
Assets slope
Into white ice – hold at the very
Offer of art,
The brimming, blossoming illusion of.

These that are uncurved
Mauvelets of wood

Know which way the credit works – too cute
To contribute, too wary
Of the wreck, the debt, the repeated whims.

The swiped reject band,
Too sure of it,
Too busy – only caught
To the bumpless sunscape,
Arms of a mirthless sky.

'So there I was
Riding along on the back of my dinosaur
And the waves housing-up – And
Me concentrating on my wet feet
(Had to think of something to stop being sick).'

The lean and taut sheets of the body,
Damped with work,
Over-sweet – with the strange
Eye-tricking balance,
The spread of the wrestler.

'And the post got unpadded,
They were so
Mad – striking
His head again
Into the studs.'

The pre-tunes of love,
The walk home,
Hot – with the girl
Thinking of her body
Bending to the light.

'So there, and bright
Coming by down
On the bikes – till the bars locked
And shot us head-over in the ditch
So shattered it was laughable.'

In the far, gloating province of the Jutes,
The coil of the wide-around sky,
Open, cogent, fair – And its buried
Sentience, bare and careless,
Working thru the strawberry field.

II

In each strophe
A different bus route.
The references are limited – But yes
It is possible to get to Bournemouth
And to get back.

If after twenty years
I can think
Where – snapped
On a scattered,
Incoherent grouping.

The rattle of the orange will be one way,
And the plam of football,
The routeing day – And then
The grit-skid and the flare
Of night-light will be gates too.

Like the many paths that lie intégral
In the sense, so,
Of a fragment – pronounced, proved:
A friend (said Orestes)
Against a thousand kinsmen.

Entering
The Bournemouth North,
Yes it is like – But
Grassed-over, what more grass
Now than stones.

Throws me.
I thought I knew where.
After 20 years? – I ask you,
There are the points: chapel,
Shaped angel, work-hut.

But row after row
The name lacks, most
Taken down, grassed – And which left
Three, four, more, easy,
The foxes have broke into. (This is no stay.)

What a loose, lazy thing
Of time-scan; and the air
Holds no more care – For
The shedding of those dimensions
At the start of creation.

So things that were formed,
Created, truly,
Exactly so – Now that
Repeat
And perpetuate.

And each of the switching-points
From nothing to shape
Closed over – Like the look
Of the Earth, all over
'ithout reverse.

Check then. If you are there,
This is the street,
And this – Quid quaeso,
Utrum m'auxilio stes
An finem dones?

III

'People, there, talk of a celestial city,
Far, in a mist, from the tumbling blue sea,
And past description – Like here our legend
Is of mountains that sank,
And lands far over the desert.

Sometimes they are glimpsed,
Peaks and red cities, so old
They seem to lean – So I saw them
In my signal night-travel,
In my dreaming.

By the lake under the moon,
To the green shadow-glossed ravines
And further – I was lucky
(As the monkeys called over the empty water-top)
To climb the slim ladder of cloud.

I was there on the cliff
When the Sun sought its way
Out of the sea – Splendid bowl
Where heaven's own fowl
Perch and alarum.

And my road was by gorges and falls,
Precipitous, till, tranced by the flowers,
I paused, rested with rocks – All
Sudden
It was night once more.

Bears broadcast with dragons
Louder than the unseen torrents
Barging down the forest – heavier
Than black the clouds came
From the waters where water is born from.

It all burst
Like a chasm from sky

To bed – And both sun and moon
Lit along the terraces
Of tumbling gold, silver.

The cloud-people came down,
In rainbow-dress, on
Wind-horses – Tigers were with them,
Playing guitar, and the phoenix
Flew at their hubs.

Before them the Dead
Were marshalled like
Stalks of hemp – I wake!
How can I live there?
How can I live here among the rich?'

[from Li-Po]

IV

Little friend
Laid to print in the index at March
1964 – I remember
The morning too,
Foggy and handed with frost.

How can a crystal
Lose its total property
Of inflecting? – Changes
Like and more than
The show.

Charminster (that bit I knew)
Plot 1, Row J,
Number 40 – There
The diamond seed all
To-lost as it struck to flower.

And in the load of rain

I am lurched to into Poole
Over the ferry – tasting
The sweet, straight salt
Over the sea's waltz-wind.

There
At the port of the chine,
No responses to anyone are to be offered – Say
I am testing and seeking
And sorting, if you want.

At the bridge,
The High One already
Chains the beast – like a saint
Sweeping the road
Of dragon-teeth.

The incipient forest (is there)
Slaps about (like a belt)
In the wind – if
It will let you
Through?

The games
Are opened
In the heath – to divert off
The eyes
Of the workers of prey.

We show them sword-battles and things,
And knuckles blackened
With blood – so that the bastardful
Thrash of the muscle
Yaws them away.

And if the body rounds like egg-yolk,
And the words pall to dead blue,
Still the passage's won – And the Greeter
Proffers, at the end,
His promised sweet cup / congratulation.

For these are the humps of paradise,
Clear of angels,
Airfull – Hospitals
Of handless grace, all
Blazingly empty.

V

So the process stands –
Team against team,
Land to land – proverbs
Serving as no way
Thru the garden.

But the wirey thorns
And artichokes
Move in a smother – to make the maze
That was handed down,
More difficult.

And the dismal cliffs
Are forked high with twisted
Track-tries – All of it askew
That oughted shoot
Like signals.

Nothing of brightest rules
Or silliest money
Serves now – only the work
Of the heaving neck
And the grooved back.

What is there but the body?
And the bruised mind that leaps
About and about – is a tie
Of blood
And our muscle.

It shines like red and white

Like gold-glass in plants
It flares – the only need,
Possession, gift, commodity
In common.

And the clue in use,
Till the very boots
Are shredded – and the sinews
Group
As they can.

In their own clans of homes,
Location
Of friends – as though there is no
Company
Without place.

No uniform but a
Glinting in the sand
Without love – all being
In one circuit
Or one road.

And the brown fur of the hair
And the gristle and stretched chest
Is torn away – the eating-down
Leaves nothing
But a few sanded slowed ideas.

Glued to a stone card
A pattern like a heart,
Tumbled too – a bowl of rain
Rimmed with buses,
Jubileeing.

VI

In this coarse circus of marble
Injustice is reduced to,
Only is – the non-sequence
Of the tradition
Of body.

And what remains of it
Describes
A past – that lies,
Is between
In and out.

Like a chord of slight sound
Moving so gently
In air – the ear
And the world
That faces it, wants it.

And the tree that is a guest
To the eyes and is sound
And a growing – and what climbs
At the arms
Of a high fall, sweep, cascade.

And the speed
And the balance
Is a bike – embracing
The long talent of the leg
With one easy friendship of the horizon.

Half expecting that
A person is an experience
So – the series
Looks like the adventure
Of the openest plain, a roaring inchoate prairie.

Where the whole season of cotton
Is just a passage of friends,

An investment of love – And
That virtually everything
Answers.

It is the complex blue curl of shade
In a glass toy
To roll – a pitted smoke
Of marmaladed strands
In free throw.

The pattern of risk,
Entry of everything
That is – just to see
The breathtaking moving up
Of the new formats.

Each cup each journey,
Goal, girl,
Weather – because
Of the pleasure
Of every welcome.

Of too the play-handed-girls
Who will wait out to see us,
Cheerfully – like the fool
Who stuck a windmill
On Ely Cathedral, and lit it.

That grows too
If it doesn't fall,
To its own scape – a land
Of flowed flowery
Connections a living puzzle.

Open too to itself.
Not only to the boat
But to the ground-ebb – the nooks
To be encountered
There and here, because of it.

Like sitting
In the world of worked-thru
Settlements – the stroll
At the smoking railings past,
We all sleep together, in the end?

Frenzy – frenzy is none of it
But the long long choice of dissolution
Over days of enforcement – and the repeating gently,
Sure enough, for the lesson repeat; and
If it is not enough it is still enough.

The Book of the Boat:
Inland- and Blue-water Texts

The Robert and Ellen Robson at Staithes 24 July 1983

The
that in the Watchfull night
passed at hAlf-punt
to Take
the secrEt wood
the blocks & Rubble-cut
up thru the Foggy top,
of the watEr gliding
gentLy
smuggLing

Ballad of Blissworth Tunnel Open

Since seven years when it's been shut. the Blissworth Tunnel's opened up. on August the twenty-second in the. one thousand nine hundred & 84th year A.D.

Sally & Alfred were clearly the first to arrive. and soon many others followed them in line. waiting for when the tunnel would open once more. after seven years' closure, in 1984.

Some of the boats were awful spick & new. with shop-new brass, paintings and ornaments too. their hulls were moulded a month ago in steel. & shaped up just like wood but the ribs aren't real.

All folk-fakery is a bare-arsed bane. and lace & bonnets & waistcoats are a shame. awful to tell as th'opening time came near. they most dressed up in quaint Victorian gear.

To match these ghouls was not an easy task. we settled for lots of balloons & pirate masks. soon the boat was trimmed with bobbing skulls. & pirate rum & chains & swords & baubles.

At eleven or a little later on Woden's day. the north boats heading south got under way. we waited long & long for them to come thru. but at last they came out & their whistles blew.

Five boats with TV crews & dukes came by. then we were told to cut across the entry. mid-course our diesel stalled. and left us appalled.

For more boats were streaming at us out the tunnel mouth. altho it was our turn to start from the south. luckily we soon regained our way. and took position just after midday.

Out of the tunnel and on came more & more boats. till the channel behind us was a massive block afloat. so we set off too. as the tunnel can take boats two by two.

Inside it was a solemn place. to travel thru the lime-hill's base. water dripped from vents of brick all black. and a spider ran across my back.

All hail to Neptune & Pluto. who make these darkened channels flow. let them drink with us who shored the walls. & made them safe against all falls.

For brick & black & might & main. have made the tunnel work again. and mile on mile its round walls show. the one straight way its boats must go.

But for the lamp it's dark & dank. this snaking course thru Blissworth Bank. & our friendly echoes are lost in a trice. as our shadowed cups & bottles dance.

At the end of it all you could see a faint yellow door. like a faded print with trees & dogs & more. & slowly it cleared & grew & coloured, then broad. it was a canal with sloping banks once more.

And here the land & sky did glow. like Ecuador or Mexico. and trees grew tall like the jungle's growth. when we were the first to make the transit north.

Spiller's Boat

for two alternating voices

A tense pause *broke thru the hedge.* Spiller, it seemed, owned a boat. *There it was.* Sometimes, she was seen approaching, *sometimes he would* walk back up *pretending to be* seasick; *she would turn away* slightly irritated *while Spiller stopped* to get the meat *store it somewhere safe* out of doors. *he was always trying to show* speed and skill *in outmatching the voles;* about ten of them *were following him now* watching *until with a shower of acorns* she *drove them well away.* Never time to play *for them, they picked up* modest loot *the rather small profit of* the daily sortie. *Despite a certain* difference in approach *they seemed quite similar.*

Moving the Boat

(three simultaneous voices)

```
1: Set us forth! | See us show!    | Let us go! |To the new port |
2:               Keep the wind | Low!      | Mark her       |
```

```
1: Punt north!      |      | Moor! | (gently in) |
2: From the gusts! |If  | Make  | Slow!      | So,      | paddle |
3:                                            In the  | middle |
```

```
1:
2: the water    |                              the pirates | Yelp, | Shamash    |
3: After-day,  | Such  | was our way. |                            They must  |
```

```
1: shall help!
2: fault us first.
3: Birth to berth.
```


Stanzas

In my boat. I live & die. under the shell. of the cerule sky.

The lift-lap. sweep of the keel. over the inky-blue. jelly (like a floating biscuit on the. Tine-man's. water-deep sea.

Bells at Iver. tonite. and who is tapping them? Quis sonat? over the easy sea.

And that the dead fingers. take to the TV. Depress the piano pedal.

The post of the Winds. of the wings. – And I fold a letter.

Twins. or two captains. – isn't that sensible?

All the social specialisations. A WATERFALL. or explosion. into chaos.

No light of my life. but a thrashing. white / opaque. oblivion. the burring of oridgey bees.

A rim, near red. a cancelling golden bar. The blurred. snubbed-candle.

scorch of a sun. for confidently setting in water.

Lean to leg. soft boxing of a body.

Unbodied. even the arm marks the. cast of the air. shows possession.

The Rabbit Hunt

First: as the snow set in the sky. Barry & Stuart – on the tow-path across
– Hailed over. A good deal of slow introduction. The garden of my
mooring. Stood about, jacketed: it is colder than enough.
Well, what shall we do about it?
Let me describe them first.
Stuart had the gun: he is short. speechlessly quiet: & mute of eye. the
head of a bigger family (all to love rock'n'roll)
And Barry. is the starker: brighter. A guy who knows about holes &
rabbits.
Once he was with Windsor, maybe.
To set 'em on their way. Alf lends them a second gun.
After much comparison.
It is already. late afternoon.
Soon. Alf wd get up. earlier than the clock. Joining them: & hunting.
like easy-pace-days: irrepressible: gamekeepers: sauntering in & out of
the estate.
Or. striding: purple with lordship. thru the footy frost. And never catching
a thing.
Only drinking: like unpacked astronauts. beer, beer, beer, lovely luring
beer as. in a magic circle. The rumour being: Stu. has spent 12 thou on a
boat. yet another 12 on drink. These are glum hymns we join to.
Little to do with rabbits?
Alf, after Stuart's wife.
Marion.
The curl & twist, the pole. of 4 kids.
She is the prettiness. of the littlest Bub (sharp). as laughy, rude, cheeky,

adamant. as the next. and every inch as. calm & clever & responsible. as the tallest.

She is the put-together bunch of children. And Stu. prowls & growls around them. like a stubbed-up rolled-out. BEAR. sleepless at Michaelmas.

Especially in the pub.

There. everyone can have. drinks & talk, sit by & boast: if not SHE does. cradling a drink. with little Bub on her lap.

And I remember after. the bumpbumpbump of the prow. when Sandra steered the boat. into the shore-stakes. again & again & again. 'TURN IT' I said (the tiller). So she did. but switched too into reverse. to bump more. My reputation suffered.

They staggered onto deck. They drank some more. They found a pub in the afternoon, still.

But I waited. Told the kids. my first story about Robin Hood ...

When Marion returns. (insulated) from the pub: seriously in tears. upset by the snobby jibes. of Stu's sister. to sit with Alf.

To tell.

To swap.

To get comfort.

Till I think I'll look in. and it's Alf. that's crying now.

Now telling her nice things. now telling Stu. what a runt he is.

And Stu. angry & drunk. shouting at Marion. shouting after his sister. not understanding. just repeating. WE'RE PEOPLE TOO. CAN'T THEY SEE. WE'RE PEOPLE TOO. CAN'T THEY SEE.

After that. it is Alf & me. take up the hunting: not Stu.

Five. six: and the morning black still!

We stumble. into socks & boots: and. Alf always has the gun: however we dice.

(It's his).

We file: out along the Cut. too cold to chat. till the bridgeway. (to the Slough Arm, of course).

Then we wait.

He thinks. he can see: cottontails! (In the brush, in the winter-bramble, on the grass-shave)

I stare. & I crunch. but and I weave. all around the waste-way. after him. (I like to keep the gun in front). I'm no nearer a catch. than is Alf. Why not the geese? (I ask).

It is (we are on) a plateau. so long as a Lost World. fossilled w/ car-springs. fed with tyres, dead rubber, shop-waste. and shot thru. with rabbits, between gulches.

Their pellets: everywhere. on the baked-by-frost ground.

A lovely tour: of. the icy flow of the hours. traced in the rise of the ground.

Alf walks by the Colne: I take the upper plateau still. I see one rabbit. I whistle for him. I clutch the boots I found on the tip. and give up: go home.

So the next day: almost as confident: almost as early –

BILL. (he sez). I WILL SHOW YOU: WHERE: THE. bottles come from.

And round the back. there is a gash in the earth. peppered black with glass. all layered out: with the. blunt tracks of saucer teeth. year & year: of shard over shard. Only the microscopiest of bottles. holding intact.

The whole shift of the land. it becomes clear. is one gigantic dump. a mutual-friend of china & glass. every colour of the painter. apoking out. And this is the warren.

I hunt out bits of persian birds. and leave Alf to the. pursuit of – and how it eludes him. and what he's thinking about. (of Marion)

I need to go to Nottingham. now.

Alf is boiling about with infatuation. All the halfpints. the short trips. the coffees. he snatches with Marion. & they plan. little traps for Stuart.

ALF. sez Tony – DON'T DON'T INTERFERE EVER. BETWEEN A MAN & A WIFE.

PISSLE. (I say) – look. what sort of husband is he? If you can't get her – try it. at least, if you think it'll work. (If she isn't. just on holiday)

And when I come back to my boat. 'Tomorrow' is moored: alongside. fourteen eyes at the roof. (if I count the dog). all waiting on Alf: Who is the charcoal-buyer. & the boat-renter. tonight: a make-a-bonfire man. ready to feed.

Not on our swan. (four of them up-and-down, daily). Not on our goose. (appearing overhead): Not rabbit neither. but shop stuff: well. shop stuff.

YOU WOULD DO BETTER. (I pointed it out). TO nail a bit of lettuce. to the ground: & wait – if you really want rabbits – but well, : maybe he wants. to cruise it too: the blinkless stare: over the way. & meeting foxes too.

No matter.

The barbecue is set. & the wood flaming: and charcoal. & a pack of wine. And when I lastly fetch. the Tarots out (for fortune-hunting). (And the 'Lovers' turns up). Stu collapses in a. bundle of malevolence. and drags himself & his: off.

Only. Barry & Sandra: and Alf. remain.

Ready for tomorrow.

THE TRIP UP THE STORT –

Ambitious. enlightening.

Stuart. has a boat to sell Baz. on the Stort. (in the Stort). a mud lifeboat. It is nearly settled.

But that is tomorrow.

The night is a different matter.

Up to midnight I wait. if I can sleep. in such a hex.

Then: the slow, livingless, empty. packet of darkness. (when you try & tire. think & work & still fail). stepped – paced itself – in: in: the muffled windows. round the wood, the steel: never looking

Till I caught a sharp breath. fought it: choked at it.

That: the hidden blizzard. the flecks, the pitted slight light. of the head. the sough of bound-in. pulse, trenched pretenced. flu of pressure.

Ache: shoulders, wrists, feet, chest all. tearing, like a way of. body-break. singing/soaking. hoarse in help.

Dawning itself out in coffee. the cold jingles & clinks. of photo'd arrest. the place: in the cell. of the block: of the wing: of the boat.

So set off.

Diesel.

Oil-stop.

A long wind. from Bullsbridge into. what you recognize: Kensal Green & the Scrubs. Portobello, St John's Wood, Camden.

Long, smooth, grey haul. with no ducks worth catching.

A snatch of sleep. (in the greatest roll. the twirl of dead water. caught, on. pinned ankles)

Awake: after the zoo. (like a lost hunt)

Tumbling out. onto the counter at night. to help Alf: slow, lone, posing majestically. at the tiller. seeking the three locks through Vicky Park.

Then a fourth.

Then a fifth. Stops.

And non-plussed: dosses down.

Telling the way – how can you: in that black?

And when it's light again. all the kids come out: in a patrol. look over the lock with me. at: What's that: – that vast. flood-low-'spance.

Us.

Out into the graveyard. of the Limehouse Basin.

WHERE ARE WE. Stu sez? WHAT TURNING I TOLD YOU TO TAKE. sez Marion. DO NOT TRAVEL BY NIGHT. I said I said. It's missing the short-cut. the Hertford Union. and a morning passed. a lot of weed on the prop. an old tang: of an old journey: of a former boat.

And sleep.

Yo. (how can you lie like that. when your arms are twisting?)

The fantastic: butterfly: mast. we snapped. thru the Creek Bridge. (once).

All day. fancy locks: and high wind. The night mooring: near to: not at. near to – not at: the Stort.

With every stretch. rowed inbetwixt Stuart & Alf.

To be back. on my boat. with the painted cloth parrot. and canvassed counter. A punt!

But the third day. leads us. pat into the jaws of the Stort. tightest of riverways. scarcely we keep from bank & bank. in this wind.

The willows. take at the shore. and turn to the water. reeds: & logs also.

But outside. what we pass in the plain of. is the softest, blackest of soils.

Fields & field: ready to sow. receiving (dark). & hedges: hills.

But the locks. so stiff and unhelpful. shattered wood in the gates. rusted paddles: keeping it safe.

Keeping it secure. except from Stuart, that is. growling from lock to lock. threatening at the dogs: goading. at the humans, in pursuit. of the hull.

And past the knocked & blocked bank. into the higher, coarser. Countryside. the veritable: Lap of Pan.

With a flick of our ears. with a thump of the foot. we come thru. into the last straight — I will disembark.

Why would I want to stay? Till my chest furs? And my trousers rib like a goat's? The surly hunters. carry on: never dreaming of it.

Never reckoning. how much more we are looked at. than we think. noted, posted, sighted, aligned —

So it blurs. even the slight lip of joy. that lines & outlines & overlights. the being we send out. (that passes forth by day)

Never sensing, never suspecting. how a family needs to co-operate.

As do prisons.

Armies do.

Fibbing about it. the hunting. like circular. with a whistle. to this corner: from this corner. like a race of questions. a probe: & sour, straightaway.

Co-operating: why — *under* someone: *against.* someone.

Making things co-operate —

Now I have come to the point —

Making things co-operate — is that how it seems to work?

My Boat is Burned at Uxbridge Boat Centre

« Bæðleem hatte seo buɪh. þe Crist on acenned wæs. Seo is gemærsad geond ealne middangeard. Swa þɪos dæd for monnum mære gewurþe. »

Archb. Wulfstan Reminds my Neighbours to Keep their Hands off my Moorings if They Can

« Wa þam ... þe ræreð unriht to rihte, & undom demet earmum to hynðe & wudewan & steopcild oftost ahwæneð ... he sceal drefan dimne & deapne helles wiles grund, helpes bedæled »

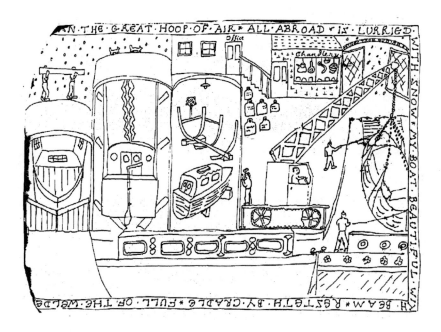

Brightlingsea

Wait! it's setting off. where? to what pattern? dunno. it didn't have to be planned. any opportunity – something to be taken.

Like in the can of the moon. we are tumbled & tumbled around. for fun.

In the city – no smoking, no fireworks, no dogs, no ballgames, no work. heck! there's an awful lot to leave behind.

Look! Solomon in all his glory. never had an army. as bloodily busy as our Queen's.

Who are they all? maybe someone's counted them properly. in sheer reaction we seem to be

More hidden than the unicorn. more sky-full than the dragon. trickier to tie than a triffid.

It's what roads are for: to new places. people. signals. pleasures. look what we've arrived in:

A field of carnival. set with moving. tumbling brass, like bees.

East coast. one hour. sun on the field. two hours. cool, the blowing estuary, boatyards & estates. each place its own place.

The buildings recognize it. being low-set, modest. Long-ears is the name of the Wind Dog.

Every animal. wakes. & stretches.

This is the Grey River. Like shot seed. the wind-boats zip them' to & fro.

So we go on, house to house. possible. meeting the whole family. that is something – surviving even.

Grave dancers. jumpers, balancers. on the world-top.

Completing the day. it oughted be something that rich. most, it is choked with rain, pips on the map, 'thoms' – thunderstorms. there are other things in mind:

A night of the darkest blue animals. of the deepest green boats. tall wheels of darkened red.

Everyone takes for themselves, makes what they can. so why need for explanation? you know what's serious. like a boat-guard

Over the swell from the boat. if I see a wolf. I will warn you with the sea-shepherd's rattle.

The Cimmerian

Parading, a parade of railings. the poor a hammer against the poor, a hammer, the poor. flitting, flight of snow.

Out of the forest. Conan, the best. leads Valeria up. to the crag's top. for up there. they are better defended from the monster.

Turning, a turn of the wrist. round the ring, seeking & punching, round & round. braking it broke my thumb.

At the top strata. Conan poisons his dagger. deals the dinosaur a blow. out of the shadow. gaining just enough time free. for them to make for the city.

Treading, the tread of a monumental quad. this is the flowers of the jungle, how the jungle flowers. turning, the turn of stem & stone.

All deserted. Conan finds the city dead. giant jewels fill the hall. ivory & bright crystal. none are left of the race. that built that mighty place.

Glorying in the glory of the böse Rose. as tho' one day the length of low ship, the long slow ship ... catching the castle & the rose.

Set on by the long dead. robbed by the tuft-heads. Conan & Valeria clean the city. leave it lifeless & empty. taking their way to the coast. leaving the golden ghosts.

Pasting the poster in the token spells. the slab of the most sweet press of sweat. glowing with the glamour of their alternation.

The Land-Search

(for circulation among any number of voices)

From the dark of the shade, from the shade of the giant rhubarb, I step out into the sunlight. The toy planes are nowhere to be seen. The armoured ants still kept to cover under the arches of grass, frightened of even the bubbles of water.

An hour late, the car drove up, between the grave-like columns of the broken station. 'Get in' they said, but we had a coffee first, & a fruit-juice for the kid. It didn't stop the rain, heavier & heavier it came, but the journey went ahead.

Trying to cut across London, no ring-roads left, north.

There were crystals of gold, forming on the socket. The hair was silver with its crown, & flecked with heavy, bent petals. The solar boat was pendent, visibly bereft of motion. I don't think I ever thanked you properly.

The physician has assumed a God-like role. From Indian suti to Saxon morris, his & her directions tend the match & point the toe, & so it is too with the throstles & the mallards & the hump-backs.

The sound whines outside of the window. How can I hear it with the beat of the blades across the window? It's not a lorry, it's not a coach, it's not a motorbike. I remember those.

Stretches of earth flare up. Brown & warm in the sun-time they seem to stir with life, there are countless symbiotic liaisons to every granule, it was proved.

Law too. The lawyer has assumed a God-like role. From Guinean tattoo-work to rivurine rights.

It has gone. The boat simmers behind the clouds. It fries the roof of the cloudlets, in a radiation of white-bright seeds, like animals spitting out a thread. The rowers seem inclined to human form, only they are too remote.

I only know them slightly myself. And now I am lost, except Chelmsford is as quick this way as any other. I recommended Greenstead, but it's wet.

They don't care. I explained tho' how the half trunks are tongued together with no need for nails, which is useful.

There is uncertainty. A tatter of plant, hardly organic, suddenly wheels & signals at the edge. It blasts thru the air, like a grand copper flag, to startle the shoots of green, & the brown-headed long animals. Something will happen, here, today.

It stemmed from a report. That's the manner of these rumours. We argued over its likelihood. The offer was vital and tempting, if you cd call anything truly freehold. Thirty foot of it.

Black and black roads under the colourless cars, monochrome with weather.

An hour and a half, two hours … The solemn lanes were continually advanced, with no sign of the estuary, as tho' it had been made out of existence. It is why drivers like giving lifts.

A poll tax was introduced. It was as though each potato had to pay for being in the earth, before eventually being eaten. And where it went to, the money, – you cd see the cracks & fissures at every hand. Absolutely, the path leads this way, past the chalets & up to the gate-sign. Besides, we have a guide who knows all this, has already found out about it. That is essential.

A tremendous silence covers the plot. The violence of the wind is the only audible factor, over the sprays of rare grass, the only plants between the track & the mud-bank.

The toy-plane smashes into the cloud-layer, makes a rift of open sky.

The sun-barque, in full motion, shows its splendour for the moment it can, for the first time.

The vast fall of light recalls the live ground, in another moment it virtually vibrates with the circling weight of light.

Locked like sky & earth.

The fellowship is remembered. The dirt of the surface of effort is discarded. An assessment is made, half favourable, half practical; the view is collected, and serves in a way, before the rain closes down on us.

In the new dark, different. Now the sheen of mud, tho' this was sea-washed, still so strong, the play thru blue/silver/grey to violet, the glow, in a minute when the light shut back & changed – we could all see it.

As tho' the grotesque legged fish venture to the top, or wound in white the dead stagger to the town & knock on the bins. All the anger of the sun-cover is manifest.

The point is taken. The shards of food warm the van and set us talking. If it was no sort of a chance, still it was worth the travel. So much of it was still infected, but that is the sort of thing you can't get from the notice. Hopeless then. God be in my ear.

The insistent pollution. Never dreamt of, the overwhelming duration of that contamination, every yard to the coast, & the coast foot by foot. Perhaps in another ten years. We rubbed our hands in the cold. Lining the road, the bright orange cones of fir, lovely & warm-looking & light.

At The Victory

At. toll-toll-toll-toll. brand & biting. the go-and-drink-out bell. to nudge them out, a knot of sailors. in the street. blackish-blue in their black. a sort slush. of man-legs, girls; sullen & shouting & hand waving. clamouring & beating-about. painless as blood-eaters. at notching the kerb.

And between the soaking wood of the ship. a proper stink of preserv-atives. furlongs free of the salt. to a chain of dustyish ring-roads.

Like a glossed hornet shell. accesses & exits. & show of supervision.

In its flat sagged hull. a disturbing imbalance. a token of what soul. & dreadful symmetry.

A rag of energy. with its keel-shit thru the water. breaking line. to be spitting out iron hotter. than the house behind it.

Then. caught. (in the wood, like a prison box). at a sudden feeling of so much emptiness outside. (No clues or rhyme or evidence of anything that might be else).

Routine of dock & café-place & tea-cups. Ex-seamen, seeds that wd jump up back the tree. stick themselves with sugar to the mast.

Jeering at their wives — . a great toorabaloos of male-ity. Salubro — make salute.

Of a crushing. mast-weight. of past world-weight. pale with oil of what life. it has left. what a sun-ghost. of energy.

Figure. a vast dotted outline. rising from the water. just chest. & heft-weight muscling limbs. undimensioned as air. against the fringe of sand or stone or patch-slab that takes place on the harbour. but promising. all sort of prior valency/victory.

(but what is cat-voiced & reticent. almost crying with fun.)

Figure the arrows of wind. jabbing out the cloth. rumpling the canvas & blouse. blue & white & brass & white.

And others. wheeling & doubling. great barrels of luck. up the plank-ways in the heart of the South.

To tree-pin wood to wood. spine to pole. deck to deck-house. house to harbour. certain & saxon.

A hand. high in the air. thorough in its humour. wood-certain in grim glee.

As tho'. it were a mere SPRINT. to paradise.

Coast Notes

The Gods were collected on the island. & would never move more. for they would never change their mind. There they were consulted, for. never in living memory. would they consult anyone else. Only on rare storm-split days. the round egg-round heads. gave like bad echoes out. giving rise to new measures, wholer humiliations. cruder, ruder abase-ments to be passed on. I do not say the heads were only stone. for div-inity cannot be measured materially.

A Dutch seaman moves in next door. he calls round for a cigarette, & in return. I am offered anything I want. like the four-hour version of his life & travels. So I take his last glass of port & leave. Then there is a storm & he vanishes.

The sprigs of orange tiger-thyme. sit at a circle, sit round the tower. in the square air. that the so-slow concrete scene. makes a packet – . no emendment. but a canon impulse forever not over. brighter than the flower-white. wished from the stems. showed in the growled growth. ended as inconclusively.

Yes? In the sludge of CREEK. glaringly claybound. dented tins. jettisoned, maybe, last year. by us, like. item: 6 granite blocks on the Maplins. item: 40 pail-loads in the Grand Union. gestures of desperate honour to the Sea. that is a SINKER.

Some barbarians rode past. today. I know they were barbarians: they had no money.

I smell the smoke. of grey jeans flapping in the fire. scarecrow'd feet. of folded-up boot-tatty & failed attempts. smirking gold as they burn. final cancelled flares in the night-scape.

Round the pool-table. there is a considerable layer of beer on the floor. where two magicians of the cue. missed each other.

The closer I ventured. the road threw me back. Whatever it held: flowers, hills, spine-tubs of trees, sweet houses. failed me, flew me back. to say. not suitable. thank you. yet.

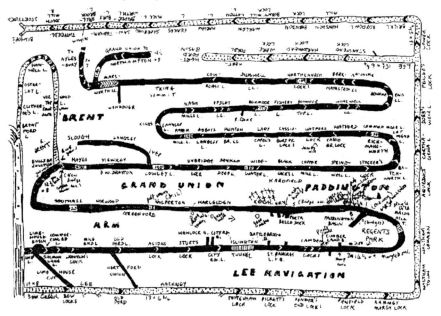

Log of the Cimmerian (prose)

Friday 18 July 86: Cowley to Bulls Bridge
As Alf's project to move the Cimmerian to Essex got under way, there proved few enough crew. There was Alf himself, Steve from Colchester, & myself, determined to try however. Friday was spent preparing the Cimmerian; with the in-board Ferry diesel unreassembled, a 25hp Crescent Volvo Penta outboard was bought secondhand, & needed a lot of attention: a defective link in the gear transmission was corrected, the water-cooling ducts unblocked. The motor was then mounted on wooden blocks secured to the rudder, & steering wires to the rudder reconnected, while I got in supplies for 2 or 3 days at sea, & at 2200 we set off. After only 50 yards, the steering cables snapped free & the boat plowed shoulder-first into the bank; then a satisfactory way of securing the travelling cables was worked out & a stand-by tiller inserted ready in the rudder, & the boat proceeded to Bulls Bridge.

Saturday 19 July 86: Bulls Bridge to Bow Creek
From Bulls Bridge we took the branch of the Grand Union thru London as we had missed the tide at Brentford. The waterway was mostly deserted, but we ran into some fishermen on the way, who slung a handful or two of maggots in retaliation. The steering wheel had been connected in such a way that it operated in reverse: also our lights were none too good. This explains why we drove straight into the blind half of the double-arched bridge at Portobello Dock about 0400 hrs & stuck fast. So, at least, we had an hour or two's rest. At dawn the steering was rectified, the boat hauled off the concrete shelf, & we went on thru London, reaching the Zoo about 1000, and getting pretty speedily thru the locks at Camden, pausing only a bit for beer & to settle the best course. Alf determined on going thru the Hertford Union & out by Bow Locks, as the course least likely to attract sceptical officialdom. We reached Bow at 1630 hrs, rested a bit & bought in a meal. At 1900, Steve left to rejoin the ferry he worked on in Essex, leaving Alf & me to tackle the Thames. I felt particularly bleak about this. Still, we tidied up the loose timber on deck & got the lock-keeper to let us thru at 2200, moored us just under the lock to fix a forwards searchlight & some side navigation lights.

Log of the Cimmerian (Sea-Shanties)

1.
Locked in in the beauty. locked into the beauty. locked in in the beauty.

2.
Swelling, the sea-swell. at the tape of the boat, tapping. and turning, a tower of noise.

3.
Fishing, the night fishermen. set out houses of lighted floats, bright floats. bobbing in the black.

4.
Blundering, to be blunt about it. in the darkest bits of the canal, night-bound. bound into a blind alley.

5.
Stinking, the trumpet of daylight. sets us moving, on the motor. rocking thru the locks, thru London.

6.
Galloping goats, above the boat. tall, horned & ibex-like, behind tall wires. and opposite, an opera-cage of – birds!

7.
Lounging, at one lock. I buy a twister, a fish-lure, big as a fish-fist. from a kid, out the Cut.

8.
Shouting, when I show the map. because of the routes you can take out, the choice of out-routes. vowing that it has to be Bow Locks.

9.
Riding in the dire lull of Bow Top. taking a moment to sleep, a minute of sleep. tiring, in the high level lone-place, for the tide.

10.
And poised below, tide-side of Bow. on the pulling, pouring tide, feeling its flood. able-anxious to accept it, with the lights set.

11.
Banging, the boat lept out. on its treacherous little motor, magically mute. a scarey shooting-down – how to stop?

12.
Tugging at the tuft-stems of these slope-plants. I try to arrest, rest our pace. startled & with a smacking sound, they start from the wall, rootless.

Sunday 20 July 86: Bow Creek to Sunken Buxey

It was 0115 hrs Cimmerian was cast off in a fierce out-running current down Bow Creek & the outboard cut out almost immediately, so that we were hurtling down this inhospitable canyon quite unpowered. Alf was able to steer her towards one bank, I then grabbed at the flimsy plants growing there & Alf jumped off & hauled her to a halt. He then located & refastened a loose fuel pipe & a screw, dropped off from the carburettor (it couldn't have been right reassembled when sold?) & we carried on more safely down the creek & out into the spacious Thames, with all the advantage of the just-turned tide helping us down to the sea. We passed thru the Thames Barrier & followed the course of the main channel pretty easily till Tilbury where the motor cut out & the boat was left slowly pirouetting in the current. But it started up again OK & it was heartening when dawn arrived near Canvey Island. At 0630 approx we passed Southend Pier (newly smashed in), but after that we slowed, having lost the advantage of the tide & the estuary water was rough & uneasy. Keeping in-shore of that main channel, the boat ran aground at 0930 just at the south of the Maplin Sands, so we payed out the anchor & slept. Waking at 1130 we found the water a lot deeper, but rougher too, & recovering the anchor seemed a real problem, as the boat was pitching too grossly for anyone to climb around the wheelhouse to the bow. In the end, we took a window out of the wheelhouse & Alf climbed thru, with me holding his heels, and stretched himself along to the bow, & so pulled the anchor up, vertically. The sea was still so high, & the outboard, in the face of tankers, so potentially unreliable, it was agreed to keep a more in-shore course NE along the line of firing-posts in the Maplin Sands, & with the chance to seek safety in Havengore Creek if necessary. But the wind moderated & we made good progress till 1430 when the receding tide left us stranded again off Foulness. We jettisoned ballast, but the tide went out from under us, on that flat shore, faster than the boat cd regain deep water, so there we stuck, propping the boat up, with no choice but to await the return of the tide. We played I-SPY for a bit, then went to sleep in the gloriously calm sunny afternoon weather. Water returned at 2030 hrs, surprisingly fast, & at 2100 we refloated, & set a course in the dark across the Crouch Estuary by the Sunken Buxey beacon, which we drew level with by about midnight.

Monday 21 July: Sunken Buxey to Brightlingsea Hard

To set a continued course across the open sea to the mouth of the Colne was not easy as no lighted beacons were in place & it became guesswork to identify the shorelights ahead as West Mersea, Brightlingsea, Clacton, & so set a speculative course for the Colne, about 8-10 miles distant by the

13.
In the black cocoa of Bow Creek. the pudding masters take a thick streak. striping, & brand the bow.

14.
Re-powered, a power-run down Bow Creek. right, with the steering working, having steerage. overcoming the canyon, out to the broadest ways.

15.
Parading, thru the pride of Greenwich. choosing a gate thru the Barrier, how grand a gateway, and. stunningly, no one stops us.

16.
Tumbling to trouble! Now we lose way again, again in the reaches, unpowered: Making a poor mazurka, round & slow round – which way?

17.
Seeking to see the true Thames channel. now at night, pylons light & line it, tall pyres of bulbs. branding the banks out, as it swings erratically.

18.
Listen – the slight sombre showing-up of day. & the massed furniture of the docks, half-missed. as slowing, we go down past Canvey.

19.
Standing stranded. the long Southend Pier, long & strong. embedded with the bulk of a smashed wreck, on its east.

20.
Chopping, the choppy waters of the mouth. as we make the estuary out, out to the wider water. & the blaring blasting tankers & mountainous wake.

21.
Anchoring, letting the anchor out. shallowish the sea but hard to see. clouded with the same clouds as a sub-blue sky.

22.
Waking in the way of the tide. now we ride on a cascading sea, deep & then high. tumbling about, in this tumble who will bring the anchor onboard.

23.
Calming, to a sweet calm sea. it seems safer a lot, here by the Maplins, ever evener. steadying, we are steady now on the bottom, stuck.

24.
Gliding away from the gilded sand. now the tide has left us to wait, watch for the new water. stranded on the large sands, step out & see it all.

chart. Half way thru this course the outboard motor definitely & determinedly cut out, leaving Cimmerian wallowing nobly broadside on to a pretty considerable swell. Dejected & exhausted the Captain fell to studying the luminescent living sparks floating by the hull, while I turned to practising an SOS signal on the ship's light. This mutinous possibility roused the Captain to action, & in a swell that made standing difficult, we fixed a rope on the outboard & pulled it up onto the deck. The sheer-pin was found to have severed; fortunately we had several spares cut from 5 inch nails so the repair was not difficult, tho' getting the motor back onto the rudder was. We agreed to head for the nearest land (West Mersea?) perhaps 5 miles away, but made little progress becos a turned tide was sweeping us into the Blackwater Estuary. So what we drew closer to was a giant bank of shorelights which Alf worked out was Bradwell Power Station & when we seemed only a mile from land, the engine once more petered out – it cd simply have been the low level of diesel – so we just anchored up, in about 15 feet of water to await daylight. Tobacco had run out, there was only one sandwich & a cup of orange left. At 0530 after a short sleep we awoke to find ourselves quite close to Bradwell-on-Sea, that is, on the wrong side of the Blackwater Estuary, while ahead of us was a formidable array of tankers, fortunately riding at anchor, like us. The captain was surly & uncivilized, but managed to locate some blockage of the fuel-filter & never-properly-tightened or worked-loose components in the fuel-pump & carburettor. At last the outboard worked properly for the first time on the whole journey & powered us ably on the last leg across the Blackwater, across the face of Mersea Island into the entrance of the Colne in fine bright weather & a clear, calm sea. We made Brightlingsea Hard at 0830 & we lept ashore to find coffee, cigarettes, more diesel, permitted to moor as the harbour master remembered Alf from as a kid; Steve was summoned as replacement crew, & made Thorrington Creek at their leisure, to set about reclaiming the MTB 'Little Island'.

25.
Walking, the walkers of the sea. at a fast pace, approach, & faster. running, the race of the sea around us again, as the light falters.

26.
Deepening, the deepest water yet. over & by the Sunken Buxey Beacon, past her. rushing over the waving buoyant water.

27.
The gibber-gibber – at the eye –. of fluorescent shrimps, passing. by – skipping under/against the ship.

28.
Stopped! stretching with all the strength of our arms. the figury busty outboard rises to us. trying not to, as tricky as a mermaid, against mending.

29.
Going on to guess the lights. the powerful draw of the power station. dawning, day shows by it the modest St Peter Bradwell.

30.
Calling with the horn in my gob, aghast at. four mammothian tankers lined up, straight at us. till I see them riding to the tide, like us, anchored up.

31.
Spurting & spuming, the lovely motor. steers us across the estuary, crossing. making for the marked Colne channel.

32.
So sure: sailing up the dark side of the mountain. sailing down the bright.

33.
Signing with cymbals & pipe. as we home on the hard, like pantomime. portending the end.

34.
Alf & boat, proud as apples. on the fine-sunned field of. Brightlingsea, boat-starred.

Variants:
13. In the black cocoa. of Bow Creek. the pudding-masters. take a thick cream of crime. & brand the boat.
27. The gibber-gibber (at the eye). of fluorescent. shrimps. pass –. in. g.

The Cave

I find the cave: rounded, sonorous, cream-slight. and low-lighted. & quietly irregular.

Somewheres the shingle rides up. flats by the side / the roof. & otherwheres the cave itself. collapsed. stops it all. I can't draw it.

Bits of card & carton mark levels. & names are written up & wiped out. token-like.

The stronger the light. the sweeter the smell. A smell of crab, weed-waste. mix, salt-pickle.

The shape: moving? I can't draw it. is. hollow courts. rounded heads. reed-spine. and patella. huge enough for … tho' it is huge enough …

The shape: sends me patterns of people moving. (strange symbols provide it). I can't draw it …

Just a craziness of cave

On Setting Out on the Night Sea

As the power – the play. packs my head. hearing us setting out on the night sea.

Let the warm gull. fend the gulf. bring & blend the air on the open dark.

It is the word of I. rare & grim. loads the trip-pipe of the early pull.

And the savage. float of rage. makes along the spiring boatman's arm.

And all the greed. that chaoticates. into the need for that lovely new horizon.

So at the loopy. gliding black. the pretty blue paint stems thru the wave.

All of it working. like elastic heart. at the slow movement into the hot desert sea.

Where its palms. are places of wet song. its grapes of sand a vivid depth a safety.

So the salt into flowers. & the weeds broached. into perfect spines of our fellows in life, in the water, like dolphins.

Over & over. the stroking not needed now. in the slim, coping tide that works the most ocean.

Unisons of tack. & trace. hopeful, happy crown, daffodilling out, beaut waves.

Possibilities of the. grand & blowy gravity. of the swell-slow pitter of the out-trend.

The piking noc' birds. slope & report it. element like element: placating, stilling, sweeting searching.

The Marriage at Ipswich Docks
(Nocturnes and Diurnes)

Being caught by the night. for first a neutral stream of black. damp & still & noiseless.

Each whelk, each cockle now. curled away in private. has shut the natural door in the wall.

Deep in the nucleated town. a globe of black hangs in each room. so that nothing is knowable by it.

And obliteration nudges each back. curving it smugly. in the broad snood o'sleepiness.

Only a ghost of naphtha. stays as a sort of presence. directionless & northless.

Slowly circulating thru the night. unable to comprehend. the nature of the place.

There is no society in this. no connecting & making. nothing but a personal nullity.

Everything is clammed up in such noughts. a sourness out of sweetness. at truce in nudity.

The knocking of the tree is a note. harmlessness turning hostile. a night mammal or a grotesque.

All the nuances are of shallow shadow. the worrying tug. at the cheated state of the environs.

Clear notes of concern. break behind the glass of the head. as though induced by warning.

And the nodding of the land. a light platform of magma. can be noticed in the movement of hanging cups.

Let us drink a coffee. share something. let us talk maybe to the kids at the other tables.

Nothing has prepared you. however such hints intruded. for the sheer nihility of the towns laid dead.

So I deem it as a wedding in progress. a burst of plain recreation. in blazing light like day.

Not so much the arrogance. of the sheltered wealth of self. at last displayed in entombment.

But more what's due a feast-day. each setting the games. deciding & calling round the public room.

Not the net of irritation. that angers each dream. as it circles unwatched housing.

But a deal of nobleness of entertainment. chucking the tea around. then happily mopping it up, off the deck.

Not gnawing at the body' store. like some machine set in bad gear. having to work backwards now.

But a like gipsy humour, dare at. handing the zip & hugging by chest. safe in being all alive at least.

With the grand dock of boats. lit up in lobster-red & schooner-wood & clear white. sounding forever as their dynamo.

Keeping at a distance the snippets of Darwin. that snarl & fight. forest up the dark.

But a broad dawning time. a slim-made joke to the girl. and tidying for tomorrow.

And the day-dweller comes in. like a boss, hardly conscious. who's kept the lights on for him.

Unities

A soft chime of greeting. recognition like a football cheer. between whiles he chews his paws.

A warmth of palm. on place at shoulder-blade. to make all as perfect too.

A wringing at the boot. a curt grab & wake. as I snag/stumble at the wire-span.

A long tunnel of wave-radio light. in/out, creamy/black, bright/calm. way-off from sky.

Evidence a hump. at the humus of the dead, they disappear. marks of hungry underground.

A great net of light. electric & levelness. and it unbalances me, mouthless for the vastness of the water-show.

A rough assemblage. wrought bright growing in fingers of leaf. ruby-green footholds, sea-wall.

A smell safe. of sun-turning faces. at their stem to colour, flower-burns.

A gathering of air-white. goes to show motion. bright-up dark-down on sky & ground.

A lighted bay, day-display. a catch at no-time. pure pause of heart.

Closing Song

The tomato & the orange check my shirt. My boots are made upon the beach. past all the castles of the south or north. the Cimmerian is the finest craft.

The cars roar as leopards in a fight. My folk are dead, my children live. the fierce heatless sun fires the roofs. in the dark we set off for work.

She will not lack for sense or skill. We will use the sky for fuel. Her hull is made of doubled steel. and Crom will guide her keel.

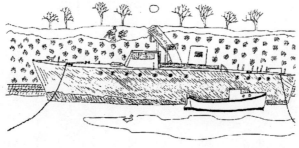

Little Island with Cimmerian alongside, Thorington Creek

Morning Lands

1: In Essex

I smell the smoke
of grey jeans flapping in the fire
scarecrow'd feet
of folded-up boot-tatty and failed attempts
smirking gold as they burn,
final cancelled flares in the night-scape

*

It was a terrible Waterfall-Sunset,
feral.

*

Stopped by the Sun at Foulness

The over-booming bronze Sun
boat along the pavement
lighted / shaded mud
with trumpets of bubbles

That we were not the only living things
in the circuit of awful flatness
back to back against
the black triangle the hull cast

If there was a deep bass brown
and a sky-treble or sun solo
it was all seeing it as noise
though we were parted from any sound but beak-pipes, and touchless.

But to be tired
and absorb the sun asleep
was real, as radiant
as the clinging phosphorous in the hull's bones.

What touches but never mates,

Gives birth but never sires,
Feeds life but never lives,
Fires but never burns away itself?

*

Yes?
in the sludge of the CREEK
glaringly claybound,
dented tins,
jettisoned, maybe, last year
by us, like
item: 6 granite blocks on the Maplins
item: 40 pail-loads in the Grand Union
gestures of desperate honour to the sea
that is a SINKER.

*

Stopt short at that (more
than) saltness
a sharp distinctness,
of mighty shoulder in canvas.
Respectfully,
he wakes the Captain.

*

Tar –
rises from the canyon-plants,
pervades the boat-air,
as the deck warms;
movement in people, too.
Luscious and ochrous
the sounds at the sea-face.

On the Colne
On the fields
Today's
Splashing level row

Brings it
Brings the wood
To Wivenhoe.
Strake with star-flower
Hands at grass-height
Over the devil-stunk mud
At tide-sweat
Laugh and pull
Work-full.
Scraping the tanker by.

At the ebb
New dimensions of estuary
Majestic out-flow
Some Creator
(Dneiper-broad)
Long-viewing the changes
Less growing, the watercourse, if invisibly.

*

Let them all be pebbles
churched into puzzles
laid out right
responding (written) each tide,
pulled round, slipped by the moon.

Would you –
a world of such jewels and wonders,
magenta-chrome, soft
and grid-bright

OR
action   (open)
pace   (sentence)
volley   (lope)
OR even
bear-warm / bear-close
a whole psalm
of body-show, blessing-share,

cart-wheel-close.

Make it salt-white-pavement
Make it pub-dancing, all of us!
Mash away the spider-bones,
Hang up apples.
I ask the citizens of Brightlingsea
to join me in celebrating
the elimination of PRESIDENT REAGAN.

(Little wolf-lights flicker
from the mirrors,
waterfalls on the screen,
as the man who upheld the death penalty
lectures us on human rights.)

Briefly!
The plaster of the pharaohs
at the house-fronts
need never even know the noise.

*

That other guy there,
he is a wind-demon
and worse;
symmetrical-cunning and moon-strong,
chase and chase is a glee,
or he boxes in blood, with
the other One manifested in his creation.
For his fire-eyes and broken-toe are not accidental,
are (product) of Another Empire.

*

A carol of wires in the wind
A cut-out of a white bird spinning round.
In so rough a night
I seem to grow hair all over.

The lorrymen have gone,
too indigent to die.
I cannot keep any covers on,
I go out, grub up some herbs to eat.

Black sea-clouds
turn over the moon:
I watch.
Wires clang on the mast-tubes,
A tanker is lit up like a palace.
Onboard they are having haircuts tonight.

Wood
and women
shouting fit to
blow a lorry along.

With legs like a horse
I keep perfect balance ashore
despite all the wind-surfers.

On the windy edge of blue clay
are racing battery cars
are huts and garages,
tough stems, fish toasting,
lids, garnets, boats
climbing from the marl.

*

The sprigs of orange tiger-thyme
sit up in a circle sit round the tower
in the square air
that the so-slow concrete scene
makes a packet –
no emendment,
but a canon impulse forever not over
brighter than the flower-white
wished from the stems,
shown in the growled growth,
ended as inconclusively.

Out on the bleached traverse
white man on white grass
to find him' god-like
(utterly irrational) for the canvas-like world.

A Dutch seaman moves in next door.
He calls round for a cigarette, and in return
I am offered anything I want,
including the abridged four-hours version of his life & travels.
So I take his last glass of port, and leave.
Then there is a storm, and he vanishes.

Round the pool-table
There is a considerable layer of beer on the floor
Where two magicians of the cue
missed each other.

All Essex is encased in water.
'Money symboliseth Life' she said,
brought a new washing-machine.

*

The volcano that was Colchester
has settled to shopping-centres,
weathered to ruins and busstops and flat parks.
And the Quakers have changed too.

One way
the Castle is run round,
skateboarders at play, beware
the blur of colour:
three younglings
scatter in the moat
with weapons, wet T-shirts.
Two unriotous slimmers
talk on a bench.
A gently threatening cat
tries to get upto my pork pie.
A soldier steps along,

incredibly oblivious of an anti-soldier
dogging him, shop-door to door.
Beer keeps the soljer-molecules together,
anti-soljers make a pile of slates on the roof as they work.
Sometimes there is a collision.

At lunchtime they are
surrounded by glittering shops of the best kind.
They will not be kidnapped
because Mr Spick & Mrs Span parade
as security guards, and
Funiculi! Funicula! oomps the accordion –
I am disappointed
the fountain is not wine,
the rough ground-flags are inedible.

*

One yellow car in parking lot / new
yellow weeds / churchyard
double yellow lines / new
van tooting / cobbled
oblique arrow / open
signpost / space
most of blues/yellows / golds
have you paid and displayed your ticket? / and
signed Deputy of Bright'sea / wrist-watches
wire-grass / selling
seed-grass (bents) / shops all round
chestnut white-flower / be-graced
white clouds / with rich
daisy / windows
rotor-mower / concert
row of 14 trees / a bowl soup
white terrier (this licks me) / music
also 2 bone pins and 18 teeth / jammed roads
bionical, near-bionical / no thru-fare
courses of tiles in 3's, 4's, 6's, brix in 3's at 90° to 3 more and so on
one buff brick above 3 brix / no cattle-yard
flint path with brown etc. broken glass / no junk-yard

pebble and dust path with pink brick-dust / no church-place
can, log, tyre, tin / a revolving current
mud-side to water-channel / whirl
stuffed black rat (brown form) black rat (black form)
black house-side being painted grey / people
new glossy black-grey wheelbarrow / well
10th May / come another year
machine-tools, tyre-service / working for a
gulley at new road North / change-round
vista of yellow wallflowers in the masonry (Balkerne Gate) / it's
poster with ferry-boat / moving
Sun now as in tunnel in sky
haze

*

Elsewhere
holding up the whip of backbones and the turkey flail
St Senex brushes the county with dragging hem.
Acres of old people
come to die on the coast.
(To not be – a contradiction!)
To wake up,
give a yawn,
then go back to sleep again.

A stopped-flute toot.
The *Camulodunum* shunts through Platform 1.
A functional little shape
painted roman green, some yellow,
red and white buffers,
black wheels, orange rods –
Not taking us anywhere
but a sight, so to say.

Also the hedgehog thrives,
is well alive,
Spinorum Rex,
IN ESSEX.

2: De Apio (Concerning Celery)

Transparent, supernature
long of telescoping legs
thus, thus, insect-stalks
hushed celery-lanes
not so superior nor silly
just very boundlessly alien
a thing that does not see us
tho' we do its presence, its outline, sense its purpose
(clear-through-as-shrimp life,
a water-air-body)
since we cannot build organic compounds
what else then is the perfect-sense
of this greatest earth-owner?

So in their secret house,
like once a dome of sky
all planted under
all silent, holy, quiet growth.

Little wind stirred,
or small water eddied maybe,
that was all
movement encompassed
and all the little horizon held
was this green crystalline growth
'our vegetable love'

        LIKE great tops
        rotted to amethysts

        like singing sugar

        as a scent
        invisible in strength
        of a wall-flower, all-coloured,
        a sun-bath and signal

or like a great wash of grease,
clinging with the tide

like a funnel of love
in smooth pink

as plum-glue

Like each other
slotted / in lock
boat like tree
like hand like colour

as is anything
partaking of –

like the frenzied radio
of full action,
no just dream-danger

unlike inconsequential ghost-ways,
nothing so personal

more like a loop of being,
a share

like the force-blue
of night vision
strong-bundled fibres

like a horizon
bringing everything into its link

like a second sun, or this one,
seen before it's seen,
people hide in the earth from

(like a stone stops it
or made concrete cells)

Making equational balance:
inspiring CO_2 & sun & water,
releasing oxygen,
and then reversing the cycle;
the Sun ate up matter, made energy
and the plants reversed it, building,
not hardly preying on the planet
more completing-refining it,
dying and returning-enriching.

And
the atmosphere itself, they made it.
In turn to loan to motor-animals
how to learn to fly,
launching and catching them,
hosting their cycles, and
bursting into flower to keep them
sick of choice for toys, bulging with sweets.
Insect-cradles;
at the first chance, co-operators
with the new helicopter-pals.

A carpet of herb in the Cenozoic,
eaten & eaten & eaten
to be ever brighter in colour.
Enrolled in a great food army,
disciplined and ranked and trained
to all level of nutritious tricks and display
under applause.
While they shaped the beings
that used them,
a whole house of species,
special mammals, who tipped it all up.

          A wind of death (glossy grey hold)
          rushes thru the toy house:
          every arch is uglier,
          made more ridiculous.

          The new Professor of Palaeography,

almost as forcefully circuitous
as the old.
I like the tendrils.

'She found a corn-flower,
long-stalked and small-headed,
wild & strong & pure blue.
She picked it & stuck it thru the
cardigan they'd made her wear.'

The old lane
and construct hedge
shows horn-colour / wood-colour
at the sun shine-thru.

What wings! great targets of blood
where a'shoulder, its keyboard plumes
row aside, like a power I recognise.
I slash my skin in graft, assume.

A king reigns in the room,
Purple and private and glossy-haired.
The angels in my hams strike up a theme
As he stands in his tent, which is the soul.

For who calls from the lupins
Who steps from the wallflowers
but rank-haired lunacy,
his local ambush.

All in the crystals of snow
the plantless queen
holds south
with her player-whales.

Between every wave is thunder.
What a chasm –
die Millionen! –
the Sun rises from.

Every sparking living cell
tuned to salute another;
burials and minerals too
chance the air.

Securely capable of rebalancing the earth,
and incapable of destruction,
being perfectly adaptable to being dormant;
unaware of ambitious waste
who are already completely twinned with the planet,
conserving energy
in preference to exploit and display.
And guaranteed the ultimate
possession
in what only they can repair
(endless working engineers)

When
mobile life
rages off into space
(where it came from?),
a little handkerchief or two of budding cotton
will give a tremble (cheerio),
(as you go),
and a vast undetectable chord of growth
plays louder,
new survivor, global band.

     all 'at's left
     a dark island
     of high heavy green
     of boughs, fort-branch …

     That sense of long time
     and the ice-lock of the planet,
     strawberries
     to
     affable warm touch
     – not all past
     but a less desolate jell

The flood of the sky cloud
on the autos
glazes my singing
all day
all goading now

let there be a great flow of grass
round my windshield legs
Sleipnir to call his aching awful calling

The same wind
I hear sea-whistling
is what worries me
when I know the braggers and perfecters
show hollow –
it comes through them too
as though they burn
in time.

If I thought
a ghost would be of a cactus,
a dead oak, browsed
flattened Vergissmichnicht –
ridiculously I walk through them.

Variations
rooted and fruited
of the great slave empire
with dechoiced men
gainless
mechanism (of)
treachery

The travels:
Jelly-pod
anchored film-umbrella base –
if we had conquered the sea.

The full yeast swell of a bowl of bread
leaves us proud as –

if we had only conquered the air.

With winter
I will eat moon-food,
roots and white blow-bulbs
unfreckled by frost,
through the long nights
and work my chest broad into muscle.

gold-match
silver-shred,
sapphire
smoke.

If there is one band, only one band,
do the sounds match too?
work-tallies and turquoises,
machinery / magical alliteration ...

Houses become lawns,
towers become terraces,
roads are a herbaceous maze
(columns and needles come vine into woody trunks,
wild parsnips root in the book-plates / hub-caps).
And
the language changes:
seeds become poems,
'conquest' and 'cheat' are the last insects, that eat each other,
and unobserved existence stays in its touch / still contact

However the seasons tilt,
the plants re-balance
winning without winning
as the only tally is to seed together,
earth-placed,
water-growthed
with fire-fuel and
air-kiss

Sun-Satin-Queen
and bronze and granular-emperor
bring Plotinus to Rome
for the wolf-sons'-city's
thousand years

Sitting by
on a dust-broad
bacon-hot day
breath like salted petals
static and distance
and floating levels,
unspoke

Around:
a thin subtle and fragrant
soul of scent,
layers of savour
inhaled in the bruised nose
like marks of community.

Ever in this alhambra of celery,
the rat will draw blood,
tails slice
as the harvest counts;
a weak-laughing;
stalk-chaos.
This will be washed,
that, dug in.

Asleep a minute on the soil,
I part
a thousand facets of celery,
look through my woodland
not a'hunt but hopeful,
land-awake
on a tiny pivot
of love.

3: With Pomona

Little home, we're on the move again.
Romany now, a chal
we're jalling
akadi Mark's orchard
be'it yellow, be'it red,
filled with apple-suns
and
biscuit-tins,
grass and bicycles,
flower-workers and long-ears   [rabbits
whistling the by-laws as they piss

*

The glint of marrow-bronze
on stage-spear, round-
breasted uniform and crown
as Nabucco collapses.
On the banx of the Euphrates
as what holds time in place
a web of melody emerges to
outstand stone, I swear.
Winged sol-
jers march
the hang-
ing gar-
dens thru.

*

quick ear
comma-around
of the squirrel
and the music is like that

is that all we are —
arrogance?

taking at others' disadvantage,
terror and terror between person, one-works?
like flints in a tin?

that there is no regulator
just each dumb self –
is it?
or each crowd-excuse
floods and hymns to a sort unity
as though just same time
were place and weight,
holding, not collapse.
the
first
spill-bent
notion ova frond.
The spark-plug is in my palm
and the wall-children
shout at each speck of silica
exploding.

a long long time of time
as the tortoise-lacquer / lost distance
cuts out / bonds
the links / a helpless
simultaneity
at switch at each breath

*

Up in the flower-quoin
in the tempered metal and triangle
loose potato-like Sun,
the NEED
for superimposings.

Root and record and branch
played on sand and fruit mulch
like a flow through a mill
and a horse on a jug,

ship-transfer-bowl.

Everything turning with the earth,
and looking so word-guarded, beast-whorled.

As of its own expansion,
By early morning
the plants had bloomed heads
branched into plumes of fire
topped, spinning –
and the whole world was moving –
The rearrangement
came into a pattern
hung with glass globes
involuted falls of light-rays / greys,
green cloth counters
spirals, together, of strong colours
with that the universe was into harmony again.

*

Like a sky-shudder,
the drop into season
as-tho-gravity-were-the-variable / time-the-constant
and the manner of this hour
(ultramarine, grand goalless ventures)
are re-collated
with a crowd of male good humour
all one in a glass.

clean, coiled limb
to peramb the forest,
sliced light
branch-bold, spade-leaf
look how leg balances hill,
hopes prey, to show luck,
or for the girl parallel, to match him.
Finger-lace, thick-mould-wood
make the tall planet magic,
even our wet holly –

what a plain afternoon of kissing
makes too, aurochs
on a dry delta,
and a wood-pacer.

In the bleached forest
drums bang
there is to be a council
of energy, openness, violence and creation
each potential by turn
breaking even,
running to the meet.

*

All the pedals are in line.
Pistons pulled or pushed.
A grand electric motor supplies air.
Tufts of pipes are a pretty and visible order.
Mathematically-graded keys
will take any combination of 10 signals.
What they want best tho is a Fugue / *Bach*
to start with a statement of adventure / *thinking, tracing*
and progress to its very limits / *each foot with both sides*
rounded triumphantly to its own re-revealed start /
(pipes & strings) not losing containing
The seeds of sameness change about / *to modulate the hands*
in this plant structure / *also a miniature bell*

*

And POMONA last
All her sameness
green as water-leaf
delicious-fingered

mast dips
to wind-drive –
the song

Fire-fawn leaves
A chatter of wordwork (something decorative) over
A log fire.

Cold iron strips
Wheel-spokes, also a span of bridge,
And a glint out on the hill, in the rain.

A row of gold rings.
In shiny cellophane, yellow clocks
For sun-time.

A leap-down of apples
The head-knocking of boxers.
Foxes astray in the stars.

*

That there are always other POWERS.

That a great event
exulting victory,
loss, failure, everydayness,
a feeling, seeming valid,
a place, marked,
a change,
the sudden the spectacular –
that they are gaps:
the speaker brought it to pattern
(a sort of charm).

Moonless to lie with a million stars
Vibrating and talking above me
Communicating by colour
Some by the fierce ingredients of their flickering
Tolling / non-pareil / boldly dewed

A power
gristle (jam-yellow)
rub-muscle

brick-bold-pink
fade-fail / ages-work

A strange spirit of gold and void
oily / changes outline
(if you would see your father, Jo)

Winding, shaking, bursting, re-forming
the fruit stars hold to the tall tree
shaking out seed-stones
(any new galaxy)
this is our keenness –
To home us there in the hive
where the nikë wings work back
overcool, night-white
playing at two-fist.

A little pile of red and green
on the floor fr'above is seen.
My soul divested of day-shirt
resigns itself to George Herbert.

See what tiny, tiny, tiny threads
the spiders hang on by

Time the damsons are ripe.
The cultivator mashes-in
the plant-stubble,
with a chugging song.

The light and colour in the tree
are articles radiating,
are dull streams in a dusk-light,
make for mid-winter admiration.
Tribes of brass sounds
roll and fight
and turn the weather into the lamps,
to make every, every bit of it
Christmas-clear

4: Interiors

Salt
set in nest-glass
criss-cross cut
why, a mountain of it
made at the coast salt-wicks.

Some thick-coated table
seanced with aunt-juges.
The cunning reflex of a larder-glass;
all the eight sides of butter
glow
like a pine-nest
or vitrium.

Tapering the fire up,
fume-clefs
enough to boil eggs,
Let me move round the seat.

The sloping cushion,
the clock, the calendar:
on the third day,
is it coincidence these three are left?

The ghost that teeters on the egg-cup
stretches, yes, to its full height
afore falling in.
I try the same myself
with the wine-bottle.

*

She is the form of beauty,
duru
that opens up
snail-close-grey or bored-hart-fawn
(if you offend the law, can any good come of it?)

lovely
open

church
that is a metaphor
sio cyrice
of debate, all the
all the stances, she is
– absurd
like pen spaces are
that waive and echo the eye
all unreal
hall, *heal*,
how he joins,
arms and arms of friends
not tongues but shoulders
I speak of the insistent muscle of good tolerance.

it glistens
like poles of brass,
this metal,
neutral as a child, and honest

and the child,
pictured with a chick and eggs,
pictured with lovely grass,
a red-haired man
born on midsummer-day

the favourite, kind, responsible,
and the dark verse-woman
liquid and exaggerate,
all for the furnishing of house
þæt hūs, þes hām

*

In a blue bowl
basalt and white
the eggs / the clouds
comic cones of ice

sinewalt – affording no entering

So heavy a work
it rushes
bangs up over the head
makes dizzy,
jangles, grows
crescate, never getting …

a bar of chrome,
a tint, a paint,
slender, broaching glow
of warm away:
not a lock, a couple
so solid it falls …

a cloth of water-chicks
doubling and crossing
they have lines and they hoot
being young, too loud
like for ever
(along, along …

I work the alphabet:
pictures that explain
or in neatness
fur and refuse …

We are interruption …

A fantasy door
silver-veined
almost a shameless cheer
that it two-heads in & out
with colossal change …

Just at the turn of sleep
that moment (a hesitation) a heart-pause,
a crinkle or sigh
ere I roll down …

*

Is Sleipnir with me?   [Odin's horse
I feel a form in the bed –
notta gross-glad brown girl-Arab
or wind-white cowboy
– a holy visitor,
such as are woven, moved in boats, miniatured as gold,
but never for that
any the more corporeal.

What of the world's sleepers?
What harm comes of them,
while the organ dusts and silts in its ranks.

Such a run of rain
s'unnatural
however gentlelady-like it arrives
I'm sweating in a minute.

*

From the volcano's heart
in its glorious light of fire
I rose full-animal,
sweat-bright and shiny
and a royal Basilisk.
I was too intent
never to fall back on the putrid slopes
(be engulfed)
ever to sleep,
until at the edge I had confidence of transport,
took me fire to fire,
ever more golden in the gold coals.
Heights seem painful,
fall or slide to some pit
of smelting matter
will take us,
while I play the same. Let us sing the black flowers and ferns
while the cloudy energy of dust everywhere burns

and the same fire that proliferates and purifies the metal
turns us all back
(whatever it held:
flowers, hills, spine-tubs of trees, sweet houses,
failed, flew me back)

Blood speaking and asking
like daisy to tank-tread
Osram to quartz-arch
But most of all the red-glares
the signal-yields
the only road of speech
(whole-talk)

The car of Babylon
so many fields to pass through
All perfect (shape/row);
So many flowers/ears
heads-high, and bugle
they are all friends.

Jerked by my shirt
– saved from being trampled on.
Another carnival!
I half-swivel,
avoid a lance,
run to the wine-fountain.
Only in the evening, these girls come up,
tapping at bird-rhythms,
swaying just the same, us all.

Town that's always and forever in one spot
As tho an otherworld anchor holds it
(Not us,
we are no ghosts to placate.)

Somewhere in the grim stationariness of the town,
the eagle
hurls his tow-headed butter-eggs at the glass.
Curls his cap in the air

And rows of cars
mark his possession.

The gum-brum of Zeus!
high anger –
The rupiris whistle-coated projectile
The superb collection of speed
we grant to the emotions

The gun-mad youngsterine
In green & ochre
turns the spinach-pump on the town.
All democrat.
(They) don't understand as they buckle on belts.

How
with a wry grin
the hunter
opened the tin
loaded pellet
checked the pin
took aim
at and then
good and floodlit
blasted the jewelled sitter half sleepin'.

Listen to the Alexandrian:
He who builds
And he that tears down
Work equally at nothing.
There is no Great Enterprise.
no revenge.

*

When I went wash
the living ice
slowed and lined the pipe
boiling cold
Once on a high and corrugated hill

dragons of anger
cuddle and flare
towelling the land wi'coarse wings
wound in despair
as I blanket me for cold

The raw air
new-day air
running like a rib thru the land
– that such energy in earth!
Soon it will become phantasmic with soot
but now it is redness
and shop-icy / busy

The great moves of train,
lunch-packs
workers once
with accents like pint-bows.
My shipmates and me believed in that town,
that everyone would turn out right.

for
I am sweetness all thru
like brown bananas,
transparent bruises,
and I link
word and memory along

Cradling a tiny model boat
I shall commission myself a stain-glass window
wherein my boots
shall be seen to stand
on the stuffier verses of my poet-contemporaries,
with a lit-up smirk.

*

coming, plate-blue
from mighty ocean
to the

continent
of crumbling mud

Pairs of white eyes
seated on a verandah,
explaining the terms of welcome

Travellers with diamonds in their pockets.
hats of monstrous shape.

Superimpositions:
of city on city.

Tainted with the glare of triumph,
the after-empires fade
to rows of frost-on-marrow,
in gobby streets.

*

What I want to set is language.
STET

Only working in the dark is a
WOLF-POET

The cycling old melody goes country-side-like
ROUND & UP

Where is their logic? Why they are no more than
HIATUS

Professionals? Ah — the little
LICE-PODS!

Misery and woe to spiders all over the
WORLD!

Just let a little Sun come up, big enough to show me
FRIENDS

After someone's death, stumbling suddenly into an open
PLAIN

White in the ice-light but also showing their red
BOAT-BOOTS

Hunting thru the cow-fields for the quietly confident
MUSHROOMS

So strong the air was by these sharp rows and hedges, as
ROMAN

Opened, it sinks, a heavy load of melted
SOLDIERS

Panic screams thru his horns, collapses the
LUNGS

The frost-ghost has left nothing but his claw-marks on the
WINDOW

Water and wood and fire are bodies, too, but
TOO-FAST.

*

What are they? They come
in boxes, they don't open up;
they don't diagonalise.
only dinky kids converge to them.

And they have found another gateway – between two oaks,
and it works if you leap.
Beyond is something new – suns, pipe-wheels,
wheat-ancestors, all waiting there:
So I dreamt, while I slept,
The she-bear stirred on a nearby stump.
A spirit shone malignant in the saucer.

A hauschen, a little home

bedecked with fever-holly — and on the other side
a sullen long sea, always green.

There is a canister of oats,
and a canister of sugar.
The binding wail of wind is round us
as tho they will not be refilled

And there is outside —
The long circle of the sea,
The longing rim of the sky,
The round horizon-run of ground,
The great completeness of the Sun;
The fine wild and white of the waves in it,
work-walls, steps, bike-runs, hands,
The dispersing patterns of the clouds,
The yielding, changing surface and growth,
The fragile arc our light moves in.

Poems after Plotinus

Peri tou Ekousiou kai Thelematos tou Enos

(On Free-Will and the Will of the One, after *Ennead* VI,8)

Is it Gods only who can take action?
Powerless or with 'hesitating power',
we wait permission?

So surrounded by fortune,
by force, feeling, we wonder
whether 'we are anything at all',
have any rights over ourselves.

And what we do,
is it intended,
is it understood?

We can rage and act,
so can any animal,
and child,
and madman,
and angry soul,
and person imposed on (to believe this or that).

'How can we be masters when we are compelled?'
We need, we make for –
it isn't us.
We're hardly aware.

(When what we ought to be at,
tracking down the Gods)

Maybe it's just whim, hazard-stuff, some fancy,
our choosing.

Or we should be moving
towards something better,
not pulled there.
But in recognition.

Not because of anyone else.

The shame and the slave
is when it's blocked
for some other person's benefit.

But free – is that making good,
that self-disposal,
'no outside master over the act.'

Pretend it's war-time,
you're doing something wonderful.
That fine conduct is made to show off,
primed just to context.

Maybe you should look for misery,
to look good in?
I'd rather not need show virtue at all.

But Motive:
'to lift into goodness';
to jettison.

Well, anyone worried about that
can find their own
loftier
word.

('We must
be patient with language.')

(open?

   (overflowed into?

      (uplighted?

         (in at the spring of –

(in-unisoned

    (in what the one moves to the one

Peri Pyseos kai Theorias kai tou Enos

(On Nature and Contemplation and the One)

If we played
and said
it all aspires up to contemplation
(herbs, their soil, and all)
– then that wd be too silly!

We will risk it.
A child plays, a man acts
both to that end –
toward thought.
But a tree?

A tree, it is true, has no locomotion;
but Nature, formative principle,
bestows growth,
action, like irrational thought.

Ask it –
but Nature sez
'I am silent, I make, I understand'
– some sort of self-perception,
a silent sight,
of splendour and a delight.

II.

And men too, when thought eludes them,
shape instead into action,
make things for us to look at,
their work.

Or
possibly
creating follows on contemplation?

'a little art in a toy' –
'a trace of everything in it'

of the everything
that marches to all places,
forms / works noiselessly,
limitlessly.

Contemplation is the charioteer
to share his prize
with the horses,
lets them
sample.

Thought we wear away in
action, and that action
leads us inevitably
to thought
– there is no other prize.

Who can look or hear
and not gain in knowledge?
forward-ways, like lovers.

I return to it:
all life is contemplation –
not unrolled/lurching to take
but a One
not all things but an origin
as produces-life is-life.

Yet
not being, not matter, not life,
but more:
so at the comprehension
'you will be filled with wonder'

If mostly all we see
is its beautiful child …

Peri Pronoias Proton

(On Providence)

I.
A world
that is always there:
friend of itself.

II.
Sometimes a soul markets itself
in one body
or another body,
or leaves all becoming
to join its upward –
universal.

III.
And the life (the motion) is always there:
a stilled movement,
a breathing (respiring)
a pool of sleep, 'life at rest'.

IV.
Thru the tricks of carbon
there is no living for ever.
The beings attack one another,
they are trying to do it properly.
Then there is their disappointment,
their own failure.
'We are not writing for soljers or businessmen'
he says.

V.
To be well-off, is to be good, feel God.

Is it puzzling
that men who aren't godlike
live ungodlike?

'Men must fall sick if they have bodies.'
And maybe we wake up ...

VI.
And to be beautiful.
And own a lot,
and win wars!
What should Providence be doing about it?

VII.
But if we are one batch,
we are ones on our own too.
Consciously alive,
Bull and frond, forehead, face,
(excellently disposed);
choosing & action can't be Providence.

VIII.
We are stunned to find it imperfect.
The wrestler jabs us in the eye,
The wolf runs off with our socks,
Well, am I laughing?

What am I looking after?
Don't we all allow?

IX.
What if God came face-to-face?
Would it be to destroy?
Sniffs, senses, thinks,
recognises this human;
for that alone, shrugs it off.

X.
And if something bit me,
I can't sleep all day anyway.
OK, I am distrustful of wild-ones
– animals or men?
'But as it is, this originates in men.'

XI.
When you paint them,
poppies aren't gold,
water not red.
Why should it be?

XII.
Do we want to be things that don't exist?

XIII.
Like a fantasy.
You lie down,
and you are star-faced,
the breast is lighted planets.

XIV.
In the undeclared war,
each becomes another,
eats, takes, lives,
changes over,
and one wanting to be more of the whole.

XV.
A dance of fight,
A war of children's games,
Where you die slow,
Are born quickly.

XVI.
And tears
are atoms, laugh,
the toys leaders-in of tragedy;
you play, get hurt, and it's another toy.
Just taking your vest off.

XVII.
When you write a play,
do you get the actor
to speak insults
of the author?

XVIII.
Rather there is action there,
we aren't random in it.
The moving is forming.
There are tunes in the notes.
A bright presence,
unification,
a poem you can reach into,
where what is the point of doing evil:
if everything is a soul?

Peri Eudaimonias

(On Well-Being)

I.
Why not?
Isn't it all existence?
Own work, own time-rate, place,
sun, and the musical creatures
that sing, every own conclusion.

II.
Does it rate
that the city is finished —
wood or rock, high-striped citizens?
If you are dragged to the altars?
Sold off as a war-slave —
aren't there routes out?

III.
It can't happen?
Yes / no.
What sort of world?
It defines itself, don't you see,
by your reaction:
sensible & bearable
& fierce / foul.
You can judge it /
it can't arrest you.

IIII.
No one can order pity.
Each still stokes flame,
self-fire, self-flame,
inside the lantern,
there is no wind working it thru the glass,
any more than you hurt it,
or help, or can go thru.

V.
No, not surprised then,
but punching
like a gold fighter
into the fate & face
and seeing it like nothing then
when you set up to it,
no disturbance, no distress.

VI.
It is the player & his lyre.
You keep you in tune,
it backs and shapes the voice,
the body you have used often uptil now,
but to work to pure song too,
& alone & unison …

VII.
Each quatre-king of house-blue,
lead-cube, clarice-gut,
helps, holidays, hopes,
from infinite-small caterpillars
up into round & down dragons,
& each shape & post-bell,
lens, little flower-love,
brute tyre-hills — everything
assumes same —
no word —
no world —
only laces, links of things,
sounds together,
the shortest lines.

Darwin's Dialogues

for S.J.R.C.

'The more the universe seems comprehensible,
the more it also seems pointless.'   Steven Weinberg

Opening

To stir the pond –
view now dragon-newts scurry,
colossal action in the life.

And each birth,
rearrangement, re-patterning,
& collapsible frame-net of calcium relocated.

Consuming work of the child,
to put its mysteries out,
while it takes and takes, collects, sorts.

Decides its labour-way,
opts how it will manufacture
one thing from another, in a shift-cycle.

Dares to point the trick-ticket limits,
scope of
what will be maximum disturbance.

Revolution of sheer area,
into sea, sky, time, temper,
stirring-magic.

That there is a whole world
in which
there are no happy endings.

And a sphere
where every feather sings
sensible, and help.

All the paths of consumption
meet,
make one point together.

Or resist,
frame ideas that frame words
that put everything odd.

View of the whole product of city,
building-turmoil,
print of new, turning matter

where the magistrate
stamps each seal of
unobtainable order

And
it continues
to mix more

make, enlong, more consume,
maximize, build, break,
and the great fire ...

Josiah Wedgwood II & Robert Darwin

Josiah: Night to you, Darwin. A good night, I hope?

Darwin: Josiah! An excellent surprise. How did you guess … ? It could be any minute now. You walked?

Josiah: A little of the way. Carriages are so loud, dramatic. It was such a marvellous night, too. What stars, Robert! I fancy admiring them a little longer, you know, keep myself out of the way.

Darwin: You're welcome within. No? Then I will bring us a drink out. (Fetch another glass out, there.) Yes, I have ample faith in the midwives myself. It all seems well. Went into labour an hour back, less.

Josiah: Then I'll start by drinking you a successful delivery. I have great hopes of this child, Robert. I know my sister will have a son.

Darwin: Another son eh? Then another doctor, I suspect.

Josiah: Oh, we must have some science too. Think of Erasmus' achievements – he & old Josiah expect something special of your children, you know. And we Wedgwoods are a great family too, who knows what we may achieve yet?

Darwin: Well, I won't call you all fools to your faces but … Yes? Are you sure? And both well? Thank you. There, it's a son, and safely delivered. Give them a moment to set all to rights, and we'll go up & see.

Josiah: My warmest congratulations. Well done, sis. And my workers asked me to present him, these wooden animals, fresh from the Ark, I suppose. We have not invented child-proof china yet.

Darwin: The others will enjoy them at any rate. Thanks – we'll bring them in, directly. One more drink, now?

Josiah: Indeed. To – ?

Darwin: Charles.

Josiah: Very well. To Charles, then, and his future.

View

This is our aeroplane
and
from
here
we see like gods.
But the deadman's map
only shows roots & water,
brown spaces,
bits of the backs of azaleas.

To the shops,
we crossed the bombsite;
brick-sectored walls, chopped room-guesses,
dry,
scanty with weeds
a possible playground
but a block to bicycles.

like a show draw
(a bow)
like in adagio,
we group to watch
an evening primrose open itself.
Sometimes someone wd encourage me
into acceleration
to prise the yellow flaps wide
the stamens better breathing, smiling.

Grand there are fields:
a long cross,
more thistle & ranuncule
to force thru
than grass-stuff.
On holidays
quick commas / sailors / peacox
dipped & dipped at the mauve.

This is the coal-fire
bare boards
the bath, bed, marmite
great bear shadows at the summer-flood-window

a quarrel-lattice
that will not show
the returning bike-light yet.
Late work.
Late food.
Late, the love of it all.

There is a fixed land for each plant,
like for a cat,
a child-map,
all the puzzled words
taking long to write in.

Outside it
is what is not empty,
but waits to be tried, called,
amicaled.

the heavy tone
blue blankness
into fog
of into where sounds squash themselves
outbeasts appear
their long coats quiet
& they chew ...

fire: what the Lord let
snatch at Guinevere
on a page / I hideous /
fire –
let lick the roof off
like so many grey bees
to fly out
– and a safe garden bundle
blooming in firewords (pyroworks)

(light-pearls)

what this/that penny would buy
if spread out
for secret Christmas things
(small, fantasy-full, little records
of what their minds said
(I minded them)
they most would never
(not even then
(Christmas) I knew)
expect ...)

And the North Country
looked spiral
with house-high leopards –
heraldic supporters and ghost-giants:
I entered.

Last:
to make one home. There
put a pillow kindly
for the elderly one
(who let me see all this
like I let me write it):
our kennel: hung with chord-herbs
and handkerchiefs of
rescue-over –
Never confounded!

Josiah Wedgwood & Charles Darwin

Josiah: I'm always pleased to see you, Charles. Planning another trip for us yet? How are you?

Charles: Well, Jos, and yourself?

Josiah: Fine. New business you know. We're a busy family, I always think. Your studies are … ?

Charles: Completed. I am at least and last a Bachelor of Divinity.

Josiah: And a good start too. It's a general degree, probably better than committing yourself to medicine.

Charles: I really couldn't. Such ignorance, such meaningless, hopeless fumbling – with people's lives. No sure knowledge and no hope of achieving any.

Josiah: My view of religion exactly.

Charles: Who can tell? I need a field, you see, where something is possible – knowledge not just deceit.

Josiah: As a naturalist?

Charles: These views of the new age of the world, they open remarkable possibilities for the study of the animal world. It opens a historical perspective on nature we had never suspected. It is somewhere to achieve.

Josiah: At least you have ambition. You would not prefer politics I suppose? I had hopes in that line.

Charles: Not for me, I think. I appreciate your encouragement but I cannot see myself happy or useful in public life.

Josiah: But there is much to do, Charles. What work there is to establish the dignity and equality of men, to build an England that is not just land and law, but practical manufacture and the establishment of rights and prosperity. A democracy of informed and responsible people, Charles, that is no mean goal.

Charles: Your work is admirable, uncle; and you have the influence to do much. But there are other goals, too, sir, and I want to discover, not just re-form, re-make – you must know that of me.

Josiah: And your contribution will be – the knowledge of bugs, eh?

Charles: Do not chide me. Even that has opened a unique opportunity to me. A surveying voyage to South America is proposed – and I am chosen as naturalist.

Josiah: A remarkable experience for you, if it comes off.

Charles: Not only that. A chance to study at first hand the rocks, fossils and living fauna and flora of a new continent. There I can learn something, contribute something I think.

Josiah: It would be exactly what you need, if this is your choice of career, as it must be if you go. Is that what you want me to say? But there will be no turning back.

Charles: I am so excited by the prospect, I could not think of committing myself to anything else.

Josiah: You could marry and resume medicine, you know. Isn't that what your father would want?

Charles: He says he will not oppose me, if anyone sensible will support me. I think he means if you will support me, sir.

Josiah: Well. I suppose the voyage will be several years? Round the world even? But you are young yet. There will be plenty for you to learn from out there. And there will be time for you to settle down when you return, Mr Circumnavigator, eh? Yes, of course, it is an excellent opportunity. I will call on your father – tomorrow? – and tell him so. How will that suit you?

Charles: I couldn't have hoped for more. And I will visit you, I promise, the very day I return.

Josiah: And then you will show some sense and marry a Wedgwood!

Charles: Of course.

Adventure (Found & New Text)

BREACH! The breach in the sulphur walls led the adventurers out onto a plateau, a rich place of fern and cannibal-palm, wild, untrodden, mysterious, very silent.

MAPS! A cave in a limestone ramp displayed whole series of charcoaled diagrams, they made out as maps or plans describing the plateau. But who could have drawn them?

MAP-MAKERS! In the interior of the cave was a huddle of bones, and scrappy clothing rotting on the frames. These, then, must be the map-makers, thwarted of escape from the plateau. Beside them, like a pile of trophies, lay various humanoid skulls, most with horns, grotesque in form, but promising great mystery somewhere ahead. Maybe such beings could still be hunted.

SOLDIERS! Emerging from the cave, the adventurers found them' under attack, with a hail of missiles. They dashed back to shelter, and saw that these soldiers in their rows on the cliff were no more than monkey-folk, whistling and hurling lumps of rock.

BRAVADO! Almost laughing with relief, they came out and fired their rifles in the air, dispersing the animal army. But this euphoria soon faded, on finding the cleft they'd entered by blocked by rolled-down stones.

SANDS! Their way lay over the plateau. Noting what they could of the cave-maps, they set their course. Soon the vegetation became sparser, and the track became rock & sand only.

GARGOYLE! At the lip of a valley at one side, easily missable, was a grotesque head carved out of the rock. As in the cave, these were like human heads, but strangely deformed with long horns, twirled and ribbed as tho' merged with an ibex.

FOUNTAIN! Taking this route, the adventurers came down into a shaded, twisting valley, sure of their way now, as they came on a fresh spring of clear water.

HERE! All around them crowded the images of some long-lost empire, standing stones, worn with vertical grooves and holes, small round camps, well-worn trails and patterns, redolent of civilisation, but like nothing man had ever made or seen before. They had arrived!

COMES! Before they could take a fraction of this worth, something like a mist settled on the scene, rose up the valley, filling them with unease.

WHISPER! Each began to hear like his own voice, like when the ungodly curse Satan, and but curse their own souls, as if our own imagination around us can make all evil unaided. Startled, they called, yelled even, to keep contact.

SIGHT! Then the veil lifted like a trap, more sudden than it came, and the valley seemed transformed into a golden richness of life, where tall speechless bipeds walked at ease in a simulacrum of civilisation, with all the self-deception of the adventurers who looked on still, bewildered.

DRAGON! Some of these resembled nothing so much as dragons, scaled and fierce-headed, but curiously human too, in their assumptions of home and art, as they gathered, or separated and carved, one would not say scratched, at the rock-pillars, for each assessed his own effect, so it seemed to the viewers.

LEGEND! These were the images of folk-tale and science-fiction, how other beings flying and walking and swimming once ruled the earth, only to be tipped out of existence, in a way proper histories never even attempted to cover.

CHILDREN! Marvelling at all this, the adventurers felt like mere youngsters trying to puzzle out what adults were doing. Some of the strangely human-faced beings were building walls round a brood of eggs, others shaping stone, one or two, angry, hitting at pyramid piles of rocks and scattering them. Purposefully, but to their observers' perception, pointlessly.

MONSTER! After what seemed hours, one stalking tall-horned beast paused and seemed to notice the intruders.

SPEAR! Picking up a lance of wood, it strode forward and lunged at the explorers. They fired, without effect or even sound. The spear passed harmlessly by or thru them, who could tell?

SCIMITAR! Wielding a massive broken piece of toothed jaw, another strange animal now came scything at them, as tho' they were noxious bushes to be gardened away, but somehow never reached them.

MIRAGE! Then the scene darkened/troubled as before, with a mist, & cleared in time to show them a peopleless valley, arid and hot, with nothing but the strange fossils of unimaginably long-dead energy. 'One building, & another pulling down, what profit have they had but toil?'

THIRST! Unlike the visitors before them, these explorers cared to remove nothing of the mysteries around them, but ran & stumbled back across the sands at the valley head, soon a prey to terrible thirst.

TROUGH! Near the scrub-land below the ramparts, there lay a canal or channel as tho' of some prediluvian irrigation. Still it drained brackish water from the cliff-foot.

DIES! One or two of the adventurers ran to drink the clayish mixture, but soon fell groaning, and in minutes, died. A grim warning to the others to carry on as they could.

SWORD! With the gulley they entered by blocked, it would have been worth scaling the cliffs, but the monkeys had returned like a line of soldiers standing guard, keen that their animal secrets of the plateau never be violated. They held stones and waved sharp broken sticks, like regimental swords!

SOMEWHERE! Yet somewhere there must lie a way out! The very limestone of the cliffs suggested paths and cave-ways that would lead through and return them once more to their own world.

CAN! They must be able to find a way! Returning to the cave, an attempt was made to decipher the dead maps for any clue of entry. The drawings were crude, but seemed to indicate a secret path up the cliff face.

SEARCH! A frantic hunt began, all along the foot of the cliff, regardless of the shouts and missiles of the beings above them, till in a fold of cliff-face, the start of a rough track up an old gulley was located.

DEAD-END! With one of the explorers covering them with a rifle all the time, they laboriously ascended, only to find the path stopped short 20 or 30 feet below the top. There was nothing to do but retreat, under a hail of stones.

DEATH! With only the suckings of a few broken plants to sustain them, the explorers took stock of their situation. Adventure, with all its chance and magic, seemed to them now the very prompting of evil, leading to certain death.

NOW! They agreed once more to try the gulley at night, but it was still guarded and the last effort of ascent was beyond them. Lassitude, headaches, painful the working of the heart.

WANT! Their supplies were now reduced to handfuls, as they retreated into the cave to at least avoid the sunlight. Not all their pooled ingenuity seemed capable of saving them from extinction.

NEVER! They became convinced that this lifeless plateau would be their last resting-place. It seemed that knowledge of this strange prehistoric animal-world would die with them. A sudden storm, with flaring lightning, drove their guards away, and painfully, slowly, they at last emerged into the outer world and safety. Later they thought they might as well, however, have stayed where they were, for their memories were incoherent, each animal they met strangely hostile for all their future, while their wild claims were never credited, and people only thought it obscene to imagine that animals had ever dominated the world, creative beings living outside God's rails.

Charles Darwin & The Sea-Captain

Darwin: Captain, will it be possible to crate more material here, for direct shipment to England?

Captain: I see you have had a successful expedition again. It must be crated here, I think, unless you expect me to leave the crew behind to provide extra space for you?

Darwin: A problem indeed. Anything bulky & weighty (such are mostly mineral anyway) can easily be packed, even the stuffed animals. The more delicate plant and insect material I will keep with me, it occupies little space.

Captain: So long as you keep the plants out of the leaves of my log, Mr Darwin, and the bugs out of the tea-canister. I find it disturbing.

Darwin: You know how much I appreciate your co-operation, sir. I will do my best to keep to my own space on board.

Captain: Of course you will. I will send the carpenter ashore at your disposal – and I suppose you want that lad of yours too? Good heavens, what bones are they unloading there?

Darwin: A sort of giant sloth, sir. I am proud indeed to have discovered that, in the deposits of a cave. It is a type no longer in existence, Captain, think!

Captain: I can see it is no longer in existence – did it put up much of a struggle?

Darwin: I mean it died many thousands of years ago, died out completely that is. From lack of food or change of climate perhaps …

Captain: Like in the Great Flood?

Darwin: Long before that I assume. In a perfectly dry cave, well above sea-level.

Captain: But preserved in salt?

Darwin: Not at all so, but fossilized – preserved that is in the material of the cave floor, the dirt and debris of many æons.

Captain: Come now, you cannot convince me that this fickle world (I know the sea well) can have a parentage more than a thousand or two years. Anyone could tell you that.

Darwin: But consider the rocks: shells are laid on the sea-floor, covered up, pressed into stone – how many thousands of years must that take? – and then just as slowly raised and pushed up to form the rock of new mountains. It is a process that might take a million years!

Captain: Yes, I have seen your stone shells. They do not look like anything that has ever been alive to me. Curious patterns, but then we find pattern everywhere surely?

Darwin: These are patterns often the same as those of shells or animal-bones of today. The sloth, for example, is comparable to its smaller types alive today – it can hardly be coincidence.

Captain: But if Creation was a perfect act, God would hardly have formed unnecessary elements and then cancelled them out.

Darwin: Perhaps they died out for natural reasons.

Captain: I am not aware of any natural reasons for inefficiency. Everything exists. If God at times has punished the world, that is another matter.

Darwin: I do not intend to put the sloth on trial, Captain. Why should such animals exist only in this continent, suitable to the tree-life they occupy? – such variety of animals does not bespeak a single, orderly Creation.

Captain: Restrain yourself, please. Each species was no doubt made suitable to its own life, and remains so. But this sort of talk … you really must not talk to the men along these lines, I'm telling you. Whatever you choose to think, it is not conducive to discipline on board for you to raise such matters with … servants if you like. I can't help noticing you treat them almost as equals sometimes. I have to mention this.

Darwin: Captain, I have seen such brutality on shore, it pleases me to treat a human as a human whenever I can.

Captain: Not on my ship. Here social and military ranks are observed. This is an ordered world, preserved by authority, and I will thank you, considering your birth, to support me in this.

Darwin: I appreciate your help and efficient direction, sir – you know that. I would not dream of discussing my theories with your men. (It would be meaningless anyway.) But I must work and work with what help I can get. I prefer to encourage my helpers than kick them.

Captain: And so do I. But I maintain a proper distance too. How else can respect be achieved?

Darwin: I expect respect for my work as you do for yours, with your important chart-making. That is the basis of my discipline, if you like.

Captain: I fear, your monsters and marvels lead you to other conclusions.

Darwin: No, there is order even in the past. But diversity too, and behind it a sort of unity that defies any explanation we have to hand.

Captain: Then I must lend you my Bible. Not to press plants in, damn you, but to explore as book of explanations.

Darwin: Thank you, I have one of my own. (It is very useful.) ((For ferns.)) But you would not navigate by the Bible, I think? The same laws of Nature that keep our boat afloat are the ones that keep animal species alive, I take it, and sometimes they sink.

Captain: Most probably if they're overloaded, I suppose, if that is your aim? Oh, get back to your packing, Mr Darwin.

The Breed

The gull pecks at the stone
yelling like a
hammer.

Things that snarl and beg:
the elimination
of dogs.

Unable to guard the world-egg properly
they break again into
argument, fight.

The thing that doesn't work,
won't match, he
hurls it away.

How can a lady be touched
by the hand of
a labourer?

All the exhibits are cased,
glassed in, to
kill them.

Alert at his rifle for people
not to breed with, the sold-
ier draws a bead.

A plate, a shoe, a worker, a pavement,
a parcel, a child, a can –
sterile images.

The monster jaws appear over the grass
snatch with ridicule at
what it won't love.

The necessity is to know
the distinction
to be drawn.

The colourful ones are officers:
they do not mate with
the men, who die.

The crowds cannot tolerate one or two
not in touch: set
fire to them.

Angels sit in the boat
as sniffers-
out.

Too old to bear children
she trembles like
a witch.

And the couples discover how distasteful
their bodies are to each
other, apart.

See their deformities: huge colours,
wrong tastes & smells & that
that divide.

Unable to discover a way in to the football,
the disgruntled player
just kicks it.

Darwin & The Finch

Darwin: Now you have a curious sort of bill, why is that?

Finch: To crush seeds with, to eat.

Darwin: And did God give you this special feature, to help you live?

Finch: Of course not. Does He tell you which foot to start walking with?

Darwin: I know I lead my life, but who shaped it?

Finch: The need.

Darwin: You are not then a miracle, unique and created whole and distinct?

Finch: I like to think I am a species of my own. I would not care to marry a long-bill, how could we share meals? She is the wrong type, I mean to breed with.

Darwin: So you are unique.

Finch: Well, other finches on other islands, they are quite like me. Why should that be?

Darwin: Perhaps God ran out of ideas.

Finch: If I was God's idea, I wish he'd made me purple with golden legs and eyes that could see thru nutshells.

Darwin: But He didn't. Perhaps all you finches were once the same?

Finch: Our legends say that a great Finch once led us across the sea to our home. It doesn't mention the other finches though.

Darwin: Obviously you didn't spring from the pebbles of the beach, you must have spread here from the mainland.

Finch: I can only speak for myself. I don't know about the other finches.

Darwin: They only really differ in the question of bills.

Finch: So you tell me. I rarely see them, only if a storm blows one over.

Darwin: What happens then?

Finch: He usually dies. He doesn't seem to like nuts.

Darwin: His bill is wrong. He probably eats fruit or seeds or something else. Each of your bills is specialised you see.

Finch: So how did this happen?

Darwin: Over centuries I'd guess. Your bill became gradually harder and crosser and better able to cope with nuts.

Finch: I hadn't noticed the process.

Darwin: If just one was born so, he would soon breed others. It would have to start, as it were, by accident.

Finch: I don't remember a legend about that.

Darwin: But if all the finches are one, at least in the past, what of all the birds, what of all the animals everywhere that lay eggs?

Finch: You would compare me with a tortoise?

Darwin: Not now. But if I looked far enough back …

Finch: Then everything is connected in life. You hardly need a Creator at all, just a primordial egg dropping from the sky.

Darwin: Or rising to the surface of the sea.

Finch: I've often thought, when I feed, how unified it all seems. Trees grow seeds and nuts, I take some, others fall and grow and make new trees.

Darwin: So if you didn't eat some there would be too many trees?

Finch: That's possible.

Darwin: And if you fly off with seeds in your beak and occasionally drop one – or hide a few – do you?

Finch: I prefer the name 'bill'.

Darwin: – You would actually be helping to spread the seeds.

Finch: And there would be more trees and more finches and more trees till we took over the world!

Darwin: Hardly. These trees can't grow everywhere. Perhaps your Great Finch brought the first seeds with him.

Finch: I will add a stanza to that effect. It seems very likely.

Darwin: On the other hand, if there was a dry summer, you would get few seeds at all, and die; or the climate changed, or a bigger better finch arrived, you might die out altogether.

Finch: I fear no finch. No bigger, better finch shall share my seed.

Darwin: Yet without sharing, you could not live at all..

Finch: I share my life with my mate, but I will not share her.

Darwin: How did you win her?

Finch: By the brightness of my voice, by the colour of my feathers, by the volume of the seeds I harvested. I was irresistible.

Darwin: To cats also.

Finch: What's a cat?

Darwin: Something that eats bids.

Finch: Tortoises don't, do they?

Darwin: No, you're quite safe. Even from me. I shall draw you though. Please lift your head a little. Keep very still. Excellent …

Steve's Garden

(chorus)
      deep

ground   underground

   in the chimneys

& tubes   & spouts

   in the sources

*

(chorus)
White milk   White frost

   The absolute glaze of a tile-day
     A woman

opaque   soft
continuous   dissolvent
form   textures

The tabular face of the scene-lay
   a walk-window
   a profectual text

*

And the circle of white
is numb,
easy-going
everything

Only the first God,
stirring
can move it:

his children turn their tummy to the sky
/ their breast to earth

*

(chorus)
          The strange
          INTIMATE
             grace of the
nose-thyril   nosethrill

the   as it
bodies   scoops
roughly   your body-
knit   scenting

FRICTING   GLOWING SOUL   MOOD

*

And
Spreads of sand
An estates bracketed with stones
As far as the eye sees
All the sea!
and its grass-top
waving with light

A walking –
A sudden pervasion of pattern,
A waking

A paving
to duplicate
the Home Page of the Guardian
(a place to walk around)
and marvel
and progress

And everything moves into patterns

like words in poems
if they stay there

*

(chorus)
      The first scoot of green

how a curl   bold
lips itself   throughout the brown
round the white   ready
hung in   to be more
          jewellism

*

Volts & paddles
of flow of energy
make work the dolls
– a touching display --
but the trees
are wind-powered

to feel the very strands of the arm
bloated with strength
circling from bank to sky
without why

So much of it, a surplus
where pyramids come of,
octagons, towers,
kings, saints, snowmen
& like immodesties

orcs & dragons
patrol the stems
of the spring plot
– flowers
battling to be first
in a muscular way

(chorus)
                    The play of glad yellow
                    the sword of great colour
                    witches of growth —

the look   the subject
since a tower   when election
excludes   is too
                       dangerous

*

The walking Wordsworth
dodging
the cues & spikes
of super-government
but makes a new plant
of so many lines-length

meting out five or four
polishing the bits
that fit
into flowerhead
– catch the craftsman smiling at it,
if you wish to consider
what's made
as more than maker

Diffuse & elegant
it stands on a stem –
only the plant
a refuge from tainted haggle & affection;
a joyless life-in-death; the mouth-drum
to silently
call to grow

Sometimes plastically extreme,
or thread-fine,
from every throat of calyx,
all / each green increasing

sweats into yellow making,
fantastic beads
of tree & black-letter,
breathing flint,
floss of gold,
pumpkin-rose
(natural ghostly everything)

*

(chorus)
taking measure

              taking sound
taking touch

           returning
self

        like a
like a   radio
beacon
in the   irradiate
orange air

*

Rich right-hued orange
area'd round
as the world-soul

to wipe the fermented perfume
out of the eyes
to be day
to hum & zum
like a toy

To recognize
gravel & tune in the feather,
subtended & supertended
a flowing of flesh / matter
into appetiteless communion
A L L

in the mirror of the Sun

Concentrating
a great chorus of harmoniums
round the borders
: surely
it must be an EXCHANGE

*

(chorus)
There is a red purse   A morning sun
of money   too red

      The tree has swayed too much!
        Alcoholic Queen Anne
          of a gin-raced city,
    & edged with the Hounslow gibbets,
        a sudden falcation

in the way   out of the way

        saying –
      Will the climate warm up?

*

Or:
after a drink –
Of course there can be no limits
Everything must grow here –
if you will want it?

Out of the terror of governing
Comes the revenge of the rose:
its thorned thin arm
reaching in to to catch
before it starts, withdraws

cut & excluded

the heap of fragments
belongs only like letters again
that by no more than chance
can come to celebrate
in the darkening

In the fruit
red-bugs
fireworks
throwing-about
like lumps of light
(all the garden-colours)

*

(chorus)
    Rushes of purple

spoil the day   make ruin

as what breaks   excludes   de-makes
        isolates itself

*

Rushing in
with challenge
quivering with aversion
the grand flag
surely
can cut sideways

And
one night
the whole garden gets angry
will not settle to direction itself
but turns & turns:
a magic carpet
with a label of derision

That is the rectifier;
and the grab and the alienation
pushes itself back,
like pissing on a fire in winter

*

(chorus)
      The blue beads & cups
      where baby Darwin came

playing   dancing
at bringing   great new mazes
everything   of co-operability
            into one

*

So all the garden is meat.
Bird-use
Plant-use
Weed-spread
Snail-banners
Worm-palace
Cat & rat
off to one side
to their wooden church
over
the dark
alluvial
moiled
grains?

But suppose the rat were not an offence
Suppose the weed did not set out to insult you
And the cat were caught playing, because it was not cruel.
Suppose that everything not only showed itself
But partook of a whole
that was toleration together,
A tremendous multi-vocal constancy.

So too
A patch of herb
(see 'edible gardens').
Take
what you think you
want / need

*

(chorus)
   Altho it is grey,
  A new plant emerges:
will it be a puritan – ?

shunning sun,
allergic-at,   or positivan
self-   taking to make
worlded   prize
               common potential

*

Then the plan stays unpainted –
There is hesitation,
interstices

Let her
read in the
ashes
if she can

all 'at's left
a dark island
a high heavy green
of boughs, fort-branch and cone
settling in the dark crowd

And there is
a patient mewing in the night.
What is it – lead, steel, nickel? –

(World Soul)?
Keeping the leopard on its back
till it tires.

There is no smoke in the chimney
no dog in the basket
no bicycle in the drive …
But the stars sneeze shut …
Forgetting to move, losing sight of self

No more than surmises …
As tho there was everywhere
gaps in the air

and the dust, the deck
of the block of the Moon
a waterline glittering with bronze
or white-painted human
capped
with a spine-pack
of hoe-black boxes

A black calendar
at last,
all made of full-stops
with everything hidden.

*

(chorus)
    deep ground

                underground

in the chimneys   and tubes
in the sources   and spouts

            to high overhead

in the rare cones   in the air

ARE
spas & flakes
platforms, links, strange
rounding power of sound

beautiful how   quite oblivious
THEY FORM   of observers

Darwin & Wife

Emma: Oh Charles, you're not still grieving?

Darwin: No, my dear ... thinking ... writing ...

Emma: I'm glad of that. Your articles are always –

Darwin: – yes? –

Emma: – well received.

Darwin: Perhaps. But this isn't an article. It's a book. On the Origin of Species.

Emma: On the ... But ... you promised –

Darwin: And now I'm forced to alter my plans. If I don't publish, Wallace will do much the same. Information really cannot be hidden – we can't carry on living in a world where the Sun revolves around the Earth, whatever we personally want.

Emma: You know that is not the point. These views you express are offensive to God. I have to say it.

Darwin: God does not notice my pen. Just, I think, as he did not take much notice of the death of our daughter.

Emma: Charles! You can't challenge God like that, it's unfair, it's unsafe.

Darwin: For me? Perhaps.

Emma: And for me. These are my beliefs you are mocking too, the beliefs of everyone, you know.

Darwin: I'm mocking no one. More likely it is I will be mocked. And if I guess aright, it'll be by the followers of your God.

Emma: But you set out to destroy them.

Darwin: That's not so! My aim is scientific, you must allow me that. It trespasses, maybe, on philosophical ground, like some winding-up of Aristotle's division of Nature, some demonstration of how abstractions work, but it is only fact and observation and conclusion I really deal with – no one should be frightened of that.

Emma: But they will be, Charles. If you don't fear God, consider at least what you will do to the Church, our Church, the Church of England.

Darwin: They are capable only of harming themselves.

Emma: No, it will harm everyone. With God's creation of life and the Bible challenged, the whole fabric of society weakens. Everyone will suffer.

Darwin: You may be sure our precious Church will survive. They will find some new role to console them.

Emma: But what? A pure faith in war and victory? In nothing but struggle and competition, cheating and worsting? The world will be at each others' throats if there is no morality but success.

Darwin: It isn't my law. I never dealt in laws at all. They're processes. Co-operation I can guess at, but competition I can prove. What I demonstrate is what is demonstrable in Nature.

Emma: But your eyes may be more selective than this imaginary Nature. True, we were competitive, we were merchants, our family, but we've surmounted all that. Don't spoil it all. Re-think. Wait longer.

Darwin: I have. I should never have listened to you. Too many years wasted. It is too costly to be silent.

Emma: But think what bitter fights for leadership such ideas must provoke; a monarchy can't survive without God. What are we to have – Prime Ministers, dictators, what – ?

Darwin: My influence is nothing like that. It won't happen so.

Emma: It will, Charles. There will be no regard for life, no reward any more for consideration and ideals; only killing and contempt, growing and growing and growing. Without our ideals, you leave mankind defenceless.

Darwin: Against itself. I am no traitor – there is no enemy. There is no devil driving my pen, you know. Perhaps we should face up to these concepts, tackle reality at last.

Emma: That man is an ape? It's unthinkable. And if we accept it, we are no better than animals. Which will we found our society on? Tigers? Ants? Alley-cats? It's horrible, too horrible, you can't go on with it. Please.

Darwin: Indeed I will. Too long we have assumed that animals are merely ornaments placed here for us to slaughter at will. Perhaps there will be a better place for them now.

Emma: At our expense? Unity, if we only adopt the lewdness of animals? Why, there will be nothing but beauty and body, men and women with no goal but loveliness and lying together. It is so shallow, it will be a paganism, a Dark Ages all over again!

Darwin: No! I will put mankind in the Sun at last. Let him see what power he has. He is no puppet to this or that version of this or that revelatory religion, he is a free agent, like any living unit, and cannot shirk making his own plans, his own choices. And I won't be stopped from demonstrating that.

Emma: I can't believe it! I won't!

Darwin: My dear, everyone will be just the same, you'll see. Hostility at first. Then they'll all imagine that my theory predicts the triumph of their own ideology, and the extinction of all their opponents, just as they always have. I really don't deal in right or wrong; what the future evolution of man may be, you can be certain it has nothing to do with such wishful or wilful thinking. Nothing is changed that way.

The Relief of Aachen

(Enter Bishop)

Bishop: I am the Bishop of Aachen. I am faced by a terrible predicament. An order has just been issued that Aachen should be evacuated because the American armies are so close. Hitler intends that the German armies should make a stand here, and defend the city. If I go, I shall be seen to be abandoning my own city, and leaving this famous church to all the insults of war. If I stay, it seems the city will soon be under siege and likely to be reduced to rubble anyway ...

What makes the choice harder, is the way the Church has involved itself with the Third Reich. For a thousand years we have been championing the persecution of the Jews in Europe; and this policy brought Hitler to power. At every time we have advocated strong government, social coherence, the claims of secular responsibility; and this attitude has kept Hitler in power. Will anyone believe it is a coincidence?

If I leave Aachen today, the Church will be seen as acquiescing in Hitler's arrangements once again, and that could be very serious after the war is lost, as now seems likely. But if I stay, I will demonstrate the independence of the Church and even my own opposition to Hitler. There was never a better occasion to take a stand of my own, than now.

So that is what I'll do. Here above the ring-nave of the Cathedral, the hollow throne of Charlemagne will make an ideal hidey-hole. I don't think it's likely anyone will fire on this building: in fact it's the one part of Aachen both sides will feel inclined to respect. Please don't tell anyone where I am, at least until the fighting is over.

(He crawls into hiding in the hollow seat of the throne. An American General, and his Lieutenant, enter.)

General: I am the Commander of the American forces here. We have advanced to the very frontier of Germany. If we cannot take Aachen, it will be difficult to continue our advance. We've captured the heights above the city, but I am unwilling to advance into the city itself until we know what opposition we may encounter. Our reconnaissance sorties show this could be heavy.
Lieut.: Sure could, sir!

(Enter Nazi Commander of troops in Aachen.)

Nazi: I am the new Commander of the Nazi forces in Aachen. My predecessor was apparently willing to surrender the city. I am not. Fortunately, the Americans did not mount any serious attack before I was able to bring reinforcements in. Hitler is determined at all costs to stop so famous a town as Aachen falling to the Allies.

General: It looks as if we will have to advance on the city yard by yard. There are many defensive lines with manned bunkers. In the meantime we will bomb the area and prepare it for our attack that way.

Lieut.: There they go, sir!

Nazi: The surrounding villages have all been captured by the Allies. It is not going well for us. We haven't got the anti-tank guns we need. The Americans are urging us to surrender, but this will never happen!

General: We have crossed the River Wurm. We have encircled the city. What is left of it. The famous Cathedral is at least still standing. We have penetrated the city along the railway-routes and pinned the SS troops down to their own headquarters.

Lieut.: There and there and there, sir!

Nazi: I have twelve hundred men only left. There is little ammunition. Only the daily ration of preludin keeps us going. We're split up into little groups now. Some are trying to get out of Aachen. Many of the troops and commanders have already evaded encirclement: they are now needed elsewhere. I have not been permitted to surrender, but today I have no choice. *(He falls on his knee before the American General.)* General, Aachen is yours. I am not a famous commander. After the war, I should like to go and keep my own garden beside the Rhine.

General: Commander, we have appreciated your valour, keenly, in defending the city, and now in handing it over, and will do our best. Lieutenant, conduct him somewhere.

(Lieutenant marches Nazi Commander off, then returns.)

General: We have fought long for the city, but the more they have defended the greater the blow of its loss will be to Germany. I would like to look and see what is left of the centre.

Lieut.: Up here, on the high ground, sir, the old buildings have not been so much damaged.

General: So this is the famous Cathedral of Aachen. Do you know, this building has been here since Charlemagne first entered Germany? I'm sure glad it hasn't got damaged in the siege. I take it as a lucky omen.

Lieut.: I guess it is pretty amazing, sir, and us the first Americans to set foot in conquered Germany.

Bishop: Hello, hello? Who is there?

Lieut.: Careful, General, it could be some trap.

General: I don't think so. No sniper's going to ask for volunteers to shoot at. The voice seems to be coming from the throne. I'll handle this myself, it could be something big. You guard the door there. *(Lieutenant backs off, and*

General steps up to the throne.) Hello? This is the Commander of the American forces. Can you hear me?

Bishop: Are you a Catholic?

General: I guess I remember I am when I'm in a church like this.

Bishop: Are you alone?

General: Pretty well. We can't be overheard, if that's what you mean.

Bishop: Good. This is the Bishop of Aachen speaking. I've stayed hidden here all through the siege. Have you taken the whole city?

General: We absolutely have. It's quite safe now. We've got nothing against the Church; especially a fine old place like this. So come on out, I'd be honoured to make your acquaintance.

Bishop: All in good time. I've something urgent to ask. (This being the first city you've taken.) When the War is over, it's vitally important the Church should not be discredited. Alright, we haven't been exactly uncommitted, but only the Church can rebuild Germany now, make it a viable new country again, co-operate with the Allies in getting rid of the Nazi menace. The only alternative is Communism sweeping the country.

General: Now don't you worry, Bishop. We won't let that happen. It's something we've been thinking over at the highest level. If the Church is on our side, why, the peace is as good as won, just like the War. If you can help shape the people back into some sort of democracy, the world will be infernally grateful.

Bishop: That is everything I hope for. My very prayers, General, seem to have been answered. If you could get a couple of men to shift this panel on the back of the throne, I'll come out now.

General: Here, men! Give us a hand with this.

(Lieutenant assists, and Bishop emerges.)

Lieut.: It's kind of creepy, init, sir?

Bishop: Deo laus! Well I'm a little cramped, a little zedded-up, but General, this is a marvellous moment for me.

General: A historic moment. Welcome to free Aachen, Bishop!

(They embrace.)

Bishop: Perhaps you would care to join me in prayer for a moment?

General: That's a fine idea. I have time at least to kneel before the altar. *(Genuflects.)* And, then, we'll have to discuss the situation pretty smartly, for we'll have to move on.

Bishop: Of course you'll start off with a government of occupation, but there'll be no trouble here.

General: I don't foresee none. You'll be the focus for the new Aachen, I reckon. And there will be a lot of changes, Bishop.

Bishop: I appreciate that. All the more reason to keep the Church as the one symbol of continuity. We'll cope alright.

General: Of course you will. This is the start I was hoping for. And don't you worry for yourself, Bishop. We'll soon get all this tidied up and you'll be back here saying mass in your Cathedral within the week.

Bishop: That's a noble undertaking. This holy altar will serve as a pledge between us today and for ever, in a new Europe.

Lieut.: Sir, your coleslaw's ready.

(Exeunt.)

Darwin to Marx

Esteemed Sir,

Many years ago I made a decision not to be political. You and many others conceive I have not achieved this, but it is not so.

You must understand that in theorizing that competitiveness is the principal mechanism in determining the survival of improved species, I did no more than interpret the evidence available from the world around me, though I may to some extent have been influenced indirectly by the imperial competitiveness that is such an obvious factor in our own century. It may be that other factors, as yet unclear to us, like the environment itself and genetic processes, may play as large a role in natural selection as what has been dubbed The Struggle for Survival. I have even felt that I myself was in some way selectively bred, like some prize tulip, by the schemes of my venerated family. Yet God, whatever He is, is one factor I have discounted in this process, looking rather for natural explanations, since if God exists He does not intervene, and therefore has little relevance to a discussion of life processes.

Everything desires to live longer, better, bigger, and more fully, and perhaps, faster; whether it does so in collaboration with or at the expense of other things, I cannot answer. To compete may mean after all nothing more than being most yourself. I would not generalize from carnivorous aggression to all forms of existence, for were the tiger to be entirely successful he would exterminate the basis of his own survival. Balance may therefore be as important as success, and may indeed define success. My own liberal background leads me entirely to distrust a purely aggressive government, or that competition can ever be a complete system. In particular, I had by no means intended that a tentative conclusion on a natural mechanism should be converted into a moral imperative, that an observed tendency to compete should become an obsessive necessity to win. The difference to you may seem slight, but to me is essential, is indeed the difference between a science and a mere system of religion. Chaos is in us, and we have surmounted it – not by political action but by realisation which is knowledge. We still war, whether from competition of ideas or gain, mere reaction to threat, or artificial barriers against inter-breeding, creating as it were, false species, I have no idea. I cannot dabble in religious matters any more than political ones (for though we share something of the same liberal background, our paths have widely diverged) – and this is why I decline to accept the dedication of the translation of *Das Kapital,* and warmly encourage you to exercise great caution in this matter, more caution indeed than I perhaps have been capable of myself.

Englynion

This one, you see,
breathes nitrogen, a little oxygen to breed;
it can live on organic compounds.

And this, this takes in carbon dioxide,
releases oxygen, then reverses that.
It builds the atmosphere.

Imagine something more complex:
burning oxygen, it lives as
fast as a fire, and grows great.

It uses up everything around it
to make it to interrupt, disturb, to be
stable, immense: but it cannot unite.

It can only build memory,
think and plan
ways out.

In our new evolutionary science,
decisions will be made as to life-direction
and genetically legislated for.

One of the new formats will attain the ability to quiz the universe as to
            what it wants of us.
Whether it wishes to be packed away in its box, or expand to an equivalent
            of nothing, or be stabilised.
We will no longer be concerned with solving our own problems, but agents
            in the more fundamental matrix of the universe.

A singing cohesion, unimagined potential!
Every last thing alive, joining in participation in existence!
With all Matter converted to Meaning!

Alternative Ending

Angel:

Non sic o populi:
Nunquam adhuc

vita cognita sit
sed mors omnibus.

Deus ipse
numdum recludit

ut scriptum est,
terra periet

et omnes secum.
Prima die

periunt sancti et beati,
Secunda,

animalia omnia,
Tertia,

sol et luna
et astra etiam

et Quarta
periunt ventes

et calor et lumen
et Quinta

periunt sonores omnes.
Ad Sextam,

generationes hominum
omnes finiti erunt

Ad Septam
Transibo etiam

Et tota materiam
Universæ hujus.

A Book of Legends
incorporating **Quire Book**

Part One

The Treasure

The ligatrix
sorts a clue
ever so many refrains
ever so many songs
to sew
azo
each learned one way
and a version
or a verse
now they are all brought back
I think
or she can make
most out
even lighted like this
shall I write it out?
no
let's keep it
aza trezur-word/rime
kind of
route-jingle
I think.
shall she come too?
by the oak-bee
where the owl-sea
points a hill-V
look for the bear-path
shuns the whale-bath
to the sun-stone
keeps in the empty hill
alone.
beats the stone way
me and some being
filing
to the clues
ready enough as comrades

and legged
with shadows
zissis the
plough-mound
that is?
that is right enough too
and it's
quarter-day
sit?
wait?
go, show, what of it?
only the black mounding howe
throws about
in the dark,
parts,
please look!
one, two, three!
four, five, six!
little points
of loose
bead-dull colouring?
they will grow
you know
now
like a map
of caught gems
of live light
of fight-light
and jewelled throat.
see thee to he!
his seams
are diamonds
his nails
cat-opal
his brows
quartz-dust
the vein-lines of laser
loops and nets with topaz
each private star
to make attack

and swing at walk
there the brightest of long-men
cuts the ground.
and past him
she is there
with every path
of bright banner
for hair
swaying
polished with wear.

I will   I was
get to   only looking
you   or backing

The Brothers

We stand
naked shoulder
to shoulder
by the cattle-pens.
The clouds
move sometimes
away from
the Sun.
Sometimes its flaps
play bright-white
or sombre
on the peacocks
that belong
to Mazda's brother.
I (it is my job)
hold

the loop and
torquer.
someone else
is expert
who has warmed
the coffee gently
into
the cups
and then loox
at the time on his arm.
At the water pump
and its dark site
the close Archer
makes right
and I go loose the
bands or belt.
Like an arc of beads
the red birds
spray up
in target
so safe
the whole field
enters
is entered
it is a sharp sort
of rite this,
not for playing or
moving,
look up
or laugh
before return
I mean, to concentrate
till the
dart is off
& I press
away lest
they land soon
I don't even answer
in the rush
of wings

being too busy
as he knows
sees
as Ahriman
sways in the air
in a pure room
of outside
then he's his own
T-shirt off
and beating upward
by when
I can work for him or not
as he needs,
or draw a coil maybe
when the main flock
break
& spar a bit at their low feet
for which is harder
till the very last
or latest
is made free
is away
with the wishes of a joke
sometimes we're
wood-sawing then
or anything good

Dance

It
iz
a
dance
(an oboe?
a dart-over
ova text
an acrobat
ova text
the little ones
that make out act
and a trio, yes some
drum, drum,
step, step,
turn, turn,
jump, jump,
to duck that
to dip in dip out
while an olivewood huntsman
marks beat
in the closed pulse
as
there the jewels
sort
and sit
deep
and ground
and underground
in the chimneys
and tubes/spouts
in the sources
to high
overhead
in the rare cones
in the air
ARE
spas and flakes,

platforms,
links,
strange
rounding power
of sound
THEY FORM
some
up on an alp
sheep-balancers
by scant green
& top-grey crops
lime & stone,
screestone
lithe as shale
turned and shone
in a tumbling rock
and standing
hot with sun
or swaying
polished with wear
brown to ground
Or it is
a spill world!
they are our neck-nooses
a sport of courts
theirs, them, their shadows
are red
what is moulded up
as by some monsters
after their own way,
speck and spate
like if the sun shows fierce
we are always
shouting and burn
and if it is mild in show
we stand back
breathe
walk it round
to the circles
of creased lobes

and
In your cool garden
laden with stone
lidded with stone
still with earth-flowers
they
prefer to start to dance ...

At the Coast

— So he found Zakar-Baal
sitting in his upper room,
in audience,
his back to a window
so that the waves
of the great Syrian sea
broke against the
rear of his head
and out
the smokey hair of the open
dives and kites
above bush-level
its barks
rat at his boots
where
     the coast
is solemn and crowded
the haze
and the hot and still day
closes the head
of each of all. It's a work,
a new globed world

with strange sounds of chords
that runs to the horizon
close there
it is
not
his scenery, no one owns to
the green (& orange)
land-summits
and
one line
the sun went up.
in another incline
it went down
distantly
as chasm to chasm
that set myth at zero
for so
I went to the shore of the sea
where the timber was lying;
there eleven ships of the Tjeker
came in from the sea.

When morning came
he sent and brought me up
but the God stayed in the tent
where he was
on the shore of the sea.
The coast
is crowded
the month-long mouth
waves and works
at the beach, the bank.
Everyone's busy by the summer
but
the high fire
and the coarse and grading day
closes the head
of each of all.

Sherds

Bit drunk the potter
boots in his own door
YOU POTS he shouts
why are you all and one
i-den-teek?
why are you everyone
exact alike; and FLAWED?
what's more
he set about his job
and so they got broke.
At sun-up
he swept 'em out –
no shards in my shop!
See –
they are the sparks
of the bones of larks.
Take the clean bone soul
of a dog
the fluter is no one
can't see
flower-size
root-ways
there-through.
Now
what bright bricks!
clear rooms!
garden!

It all seemed too
easy there
only too
that same easiness
he said
that's
bringing them up
attached
like

for totting up
as last year
I give-give
four palms
20 fingers
like a hedgehog
and let distribute them they.
Laid out
left aside
the pockitid
seeds off
of balsam
zip and zip
are triggers some
rockets
and fire ash
more and
here the chest will arch
the spine rise nearly, it is
what blocks the shoulders
up to width and strength
like how I grow
and the air
busy
between the shoulders, shrugs –
what a level, even place it is
these targets!
but the useful
citizens!
like some
today
exculpates
(in anything) and the yards
and squared rooms
thinking
like the wires in a watch.
When the new house
was achieved
what bright bricks!
clear rooms!

garden!
it all seemed so
strange there
only too that same newness
was pleasing
to see
and every plant
began
to cast its
ropes up
with a joke ...

Ra

The edge of the world.
A sad-enough place.
There SNOW SNOW SNOW
so go home NOW
say the police.
Time/time lots
to invoke
stand back
from the breves of growth
the clutes
the plates of card
that flap at the coin-doors
along the land of the east
like ice.
Unlike, like too
the flowing walls of chalk
face up,

or vault or slide
where echoes are upwritten
that are signs of sleep
(not taking) –
a vessel
a lamp
a boat
a pot
: signs, unsettled.
Unguarded
after the noon.
Grey is the gob
of the hatking
whose heart
is godbig
ribs chime
in the zinc
(the sky)
before he kicks the cliffs
hymns shake loose
and slated sun-chips
there
the slant of the salmon
the twisted, white clouds
divide the sun
into multi-shafts
and wind sides it here and there
the grey mazes and glass palaces
(as something good)
speak
I would like to be Sun-God
as I too.
On the slope
the God who is crocodile
slides at the floor of carnelian
(Stronger-than-the-mountain is his name)
you see him
turn his gaze
upon the Sun in its Sun-Barque
for then the crew halt their oars

and their dizziness has interrupted
                    the completion of it ...
not any other, no
recognizing only what
himself put into someone else
(to give up than share?
No! no! it ought to share!)
no collectors of, of
the breves of growth
in claustra
as pure cells of giant Bee
watching
that heaven with light did fill
the spaces
half footing
half vacant with
brazen scales
as hollow as
his æry plumes
tighted as
roused scales
that cap and rattle the cells of
his flaggy wing
knocking by and by as boxes
of hollow blowing
held in the air in
thick entangled knots
and on his back the
shields of red
the rimes of stems
deadly sharp
for
then the crew halted their oars
and their dizziness interrupted
                    the completion of it

below was a roar and a running of fire
a red net in the night

On the Nile

And when the Kings are moved
And when there is no one left to cry to!
From the caves high in the air
the government has taken them
back to their barges on the Nile.
Through the grey-hung lime
the peachey-horn-sun canyon
they move
before the cries of their keepers
who scarcely console
how the jet-eared jackal
stabs and drags him with them.
There is a loop of outcry over the sky.
To lose a secret
to tip up a God.
To be woken, shook awake, after such sleep.
Ceasing to be 'The People'.
To create lack.
The pert-gunned boats
are nothing but this.
There is disturbance
in the scale of the sky.
They provoke such sound,
for their orderliness of labels.
Judging
the silliness of wrong hands
the black-sided patron of the dead
lifts his evening fur,
and becomes the watcher of the crime
as he limps
and lips his great teeth.
In the pause of a century,
his shadow moves from
one rock to the next,
more sure than any war/idea
that hunt for restitution.
His news is the echo

of a lament
already old,
already away.

The sweart air disbands
and the
fields are shared with people
icon-things of chalk and hedge
lapping with the cattle
in a sturdy road of bright,
all-feeding air.
There
the greater eye of Horus
is safely lodged
that shan't be lost
(loan, keep, show, or share?)
burning bright
in the arm and arch
smiling
all – round and round
that the dog-nod trees
bend their limbs
wag their roots
discomfortedly
they have no hoard of hymns
but black mines
of bowls of coal
and the flags
weave and rock
with every bolt
that stirs the sun
sends the roads and door-patches
flaring about us
into
like lanes of terror
for begging out the adventure bits.
So stopped.
till …
Then it is Seth who has to turn that way
and show himself

so then that the stages apart
can see it
and get safely on

forces the final eyes shut

holding to no-one

Part Two

The Argosy

Jason –
gold then almond
shone his puppet dress
against the grove-pattern.
A lover
that was his part
in the quest-sail

Gems
if they had djinns in them
sending out light
a fist-diamond
watery as a pear
light-sliced pink

Out in the rime
the ribs of ice-jokes
gem in the tarmac.
I taste ferrous air.
They are frozen, they are solid
all the stinks of London.
Landless dragons
deal out ugly rumours, all the same.
Or savager.

Like a dragon-quilt
my grass-scape, cress, aylett, & beside the water, comfrey,
'why it's like a walk in paradise'
say 2 gipsies, for our benefit,
as they're off to hatch a plot on some boat.
Yes, snake-neighbours,
let me hang the winter-tree with yellow bottles
not spells (love-worked moorings), folk,
to make you perfect,
just bearable.

It is fifty-three.   The land floods.
Then the great lady   left her estate of dead birds
sped south   to screen her cognizance
for the deity denies evil   won't be delivered to bad luck.
Who would choose mud   above chalcedonies?
Who would not eat   exquisitely, talk in angel-speech
pretend there is nothing,   no weather?

I look in the crazy mirror
  it is fluid and thoughtless
    some are tigers' claws, combats, clouds,
      panniers of oats, all ugly, blowing and blown.

great break / burst of oil
searing the hot cylinder / the cylinder ribs
black cape on the shoulder tips
   age-dust to forearms
      shadowing the jeans
welding and bike and owner
its heavy carbon
all but life-holding
grease-coat and oil-hymn

Comets & star-pops
curl from my cigarette;
it is possible they will all be souls.

The purpose: glory of the word
The purpose: human sense together
The purpose: futures
The purpose: all how we work
Also: dinner-plates, laughs & fashions,
The patterns! & their erotic force.

Poised
to take a peach,
tho the studs of it prove skull-stones.
Locks that won't turn.
Snapped flower-threads.
Wd not, wd not

walk up
empty stairs
stairs from the bed
and the sea-bed

The seeds of peace
stirred into the fertile furrow.

The mud-million
slowly and slowly mo' imperfe't
re-forming
re-growing (unshowing)
slowing

A taint carpet
A music-wheel racheting over the shop
(sez) Will you buy me?

At the walk of the beast
the padding knife-plants turn, wait, acknowledge
and the woh-spined fox family, sods though,
sneer and slow and superior,
how the taddy-lights
marvel the spire-stand-grass.
It is shrieking, its pass
– who guesses what the hunter has ahead?

Pattern-Peeps

cute eight yellow-lions
biscuit-edged on the petals
outstanding the song of hum of interference

so to cross water
the Ninja if he shows himself
gums on leaves (skin-scales)
walks on wood-shoes over the river-top.
Look, like a word, he isn't visible.

the turquoise sugar-stain,
the yellow eyes:
toads, adders, spike-newts
spell out local adverts, in nature-breaks

AMERICA
discovers itself
to be homosexual!
with little pockets
of
bisexuality

There are flaring blue cups of coal
deep streamers of mauve
in the diesel

Turn the wires:
there are great laid-dryer fields of brix
burning redder,
shifts, tans, 'sort of super-carrot'

Droitly the whale-hunter
weighs the focus
& centres on
a snowflake

Everything moves into pattern

like words in poetry
(tho few enuf stay there)

It switches /
buttons flash /
there is the unmistakable odour of authority
& cheap silver forks

death spinel –
flack.
The great cake of the city endensens itself.

And we dodge,
dodge
and the pinball track
and the cellotape-trumpet-board rounds / hems it all so lovely

Brunnhilde & Me

cartoon beauty
the children's world of Wagner
sequin-chatter / double-glassed
and the ardour of quest
mazed between green frost-trees
book-cliffs
sun-coloured clouds.
Our arms with the softness of bread
hold & hold

hooper-squawk
grit-tufts
crystal-twinning wings
sand-mat and bristly
a bird
        to announce

the secrets of language
think-gloat and deep-glass
charm-conversant,
                              whole

Echo
with both hands
trap-carrots the conscious-ty.
a circle of time
re-rehearsed and re-re-rehearsed
in continuity
a rhyme-road
super-emotioned, drunken, heroic

A path between square-lights
sloping, beamed,
sun-wood once and coal-headed
a twisted child-show of Pinner,
once light-skewed, again
a shade-shop
and the planes broad and hot
art-stopped
then crooked in a fairy-wail.

Still it snows
and between the boulder-grains
on the roots,
dragon-lice and worm-hunters
shoulder-off soil.
There are challenges,
a hunting horn.

Word-real
repeat magic
all real-access
points that graph a meaning
more wonder
when the stones & larch-foxes listen,
carry,
show.

Thru the move of words,
the course-music,
attainment,
a rachet, renown
a dissolving salt on finger
of a future,
only
that links, makes broad, connects

At last
the radio-head
booms in Mithras-field

flutes the air
across to each other.
The idea is a light,
a town of invisible arrows
moulding its beaks pleasantly,
a culture-shatter;
not just the mask of movement,
but a new territory,
where the running grinning notes
fall in ver-romance,
ready-rent,
like all walls gates
wires roads.

Metamorphoses

The glorying brass band
be's rodent jaun-
gobbed, fur-button:
there is a throat-roar, the
pleasure of the summer state.

The river-run
pours from its heart,
pools, re-cycles,
brandishing its diploma (new transparency)
then works from bright to silt
moving, then slowing,
flooding, falling,
holding round the whole land.

In arms,
she is medal'd into something special,
more wood
more baumgeist
more colour-sprint, spectacularly dumb!

Breathing
& cheek on clover
its own sweet green chew pervades the system.
I can wipe out my man-scent by it,
be all growth
exchange
calm-grin, sumptuously grand!

But not the truth.
more
some German forest-thing –
a pineapple or a panther.

The Ship

I am whale-in.
Ribs reach them over-across
We built them shaped so,
for a lovely roof
ply'ed
lined
plum-resin-soak to save wood
and it is all a fools' ship
so gross the water
and the rain lies.

Raw
we rub chest with chest
to be tribes that spark
whose the tubes / veins
inter-ring and branch us
thru

These are the chords, the crowd,
the hot hymn singing
that the ships should sail
gauze-mauve
white-lemon
life-links

Something is missing:
foam poem
which is layers & layers
sun-bright and crumb-likest.

I do not mean
great house-side-size pearls
but the tiny-ortant
          seeds of democracy

To be no arch of the church,
piddle-state,

no shaper, cut grave of the hill
(slicescape)
at all but

To dwindle
            : nought
to lack name / 'nown
leave nothing.
Isn't that?
(jus'
dandy)

Tracking the Bear

Tree-glint
steel windless day (still)
and (I amble up)
snow-scent

somewhere
the bear
rubs its'
on the riven fluted bark —
handle the hair
coarse dark or silky white

There's a singing
of icicles and twigs
as I up thru the brush.
Here is
soiled snow.

Humpy and uneven ground.
What I done
I rolled almost
into the glade
to face the bear
dancing softly on shaggy-over paws
with lovely phrases to mouthe.

All is
noticing,
not alarmed.
Stood then
chest-wall to chest
with breath-pattern talk

Or
not wanting to think more
(so icy)
we embrace.

There
This is how I configure It:
tiny palace-works
architected: quartzed-up twigs of snow,
gulfs, tunnels,
gaps, melt-spaces, blu windows
a cold-quiet paradise
I meet in

All the time,
I love.
It isn't a history (or narrative),
altogether more something present,
in which the waterscape is as clear
as body.

Has tones, touches,
tests and attitudes, tastes.
And there are rolling waltzes there
mark total trust.

They are arrogant, are themselves.
Are separate, like air / lung
And in the decomposing,
warming war,
before I can magnify a pattern,
they merge
(Never
unsonorous).

coffee-branch-scent body
warm, inhaling nearness
& our brokenness
and growth

Siegfried and Me

Test!

how, for dark,
like lights and live in the wire,
the grass, the up-threads, a little burns
(a close, cool flame)
to lie and watch it.

And
by the grand desk of snow,
bleak tree-penned, under:
unnaturally, in order,
as ultra-violet the GLOW
of some unique new-up flower
itself-shone.

A big dance
of this / that branch
blowing / bellowing / careering
out of the worm-path;
green-blooded oak-stemmed
wavure, for regret of
the gold beast –
such nets of wood-light.

And
dark-hue-weave
mute-blend
I cloth-shred me,
I lick my sweat off of the fight,
en-tube me, ribs to black T-shirt,
clothes & clings to the red,
grey-shirt mine on,
stiff, body-braider,
and black bull-jacket, glossed, fringed,
black-jeaned.
Victory.

And each morning,
a trail of horror round us,
when ghosts pass, we are,
Notes
of THIS chaos,
THIS coincidence,
world-flares, world-spots,
sudden things & corona,
grab / keep / collect (connect to us).

Adventure:
our own veins' work,
VIA, POPULUS,
CAPUT DRACONIS

That lovely adherence
(that LOVE)

Till left in stone,
cooler Time
adjusts, sets us,
losses out, ungangs
the gorgeous act-smell, place-glue
one-to-all urgency,
private laughing hero-self bless & sure-way
– all blown by.
flat decomposition (goodbye).

Coal

1

Let chisel catch coal
be beauty,
undercut
shine under.

A great work!
A hollow tower,
dark-storey on black nave
glimpsey side-chapel.
This is all inverse.

And the cutter,
chest-engine,
to disturb
the lie, the bed –
dust all air.

See what man has made!
Un-world,
reckless space.
Some long-lasting negative,
everly one side of sign,
a brand great optimism –
colour-trees, palace-town,
the glove of all-light.

Or a cup dropped.

Honeycomb here
is in that place hills.
They load the sea up
with land.

Ah, you loser.

You have not seen
the labyrinth.

A celery-centre
dun-crystall'd and fixed
and shadeless core.

The open altar
and coal-heart.

*

Sea-coal
is coal by sea.

Family is
these and these,
not a more,
but same,
you soldiers,
lads and ladies,
a letter-lode
for the matrix.

See the seam,
scorched with its moving,
and a long map.

Justitia they heaved out,
and Rhetorica.
Laetitia, keeper of
the lunch-box.

Interiminally
the camels of coal
hump up and
up the colon,
looking to retch something,
make food in the sun.

Who shapes the coal?
The buns and rock-pheasants,
ham-rolls and plate-rifts.

(there is no time,
taken in it)

This emerges,
that you can search the mould,
see what it makes.

Take out
the tin-demon,
throw it at its god,
smash the up-frame.
Abstract, denial of world.

Whims.
Sit back, observe the joker,
dealing out lists of things
to be credited.
Great pay.

Maybe the horse-box
and the Ark
collect a bit of peace,
or the long long galleries.

*

The style is this
first bell-pits
and adits
glazed into the brow hill-side,
and then
vertical shaft
lined iron.

Look,
the closer you get,
the more light-like
each other,
nobilmente.
The axe-juice

spark-ark
which burns.

Blows the
corn-shelf,
saddle, candle, truck.
Late in the strata,
a tamarind.

Quick banjo,
play to law,
crumble, slough down, slide,
know flat.

Time-terror,
over the cattle,
a word-threat,
glue-game-web.

Unworst,
triples its sky,
best bowl.

And self-names
of Bee-Wolf,
God-Gave,
Petal,
crown the sea-bank.

Idea
and shape of paper.

Light-down,
Night-thistle.

*

A marvel
of industrial archaeology.

(How it grew)

One sort of ab-use
one rounding it
(more like it ought to sound).

Then the trains.
Link, arrangement, movement;
brightly-banded commas
click up.

Metaphors
accusing you of
wholesale cheating.

Drownéd
in rhythm,
tune,
say-on,
rout,
and win.

Slap-happy,
observator of some
Irminsul, 'immense pillar'
which projects the sky,
saves the roof,
alarms, exclaims, is male-noun and most.

And some are
rounded and act,
shift, all-liquid
planets of endless sea,
useless to anchor.

Keeps its sail,
its line
stitch,
columns,
time,

marks of.

*

In his sleep
he was still
sprinting, kneeling, wending.

'The moneyboy
and the moneygirl'
in a little dish – and others
'only weird fauna of the coal-seams'

Spot-patterns
gaudy, fungoid,
land-gold
trim the shirt / the dress
bind the barge / the bridge

and a sight:
fire on water!

these are the coal-barges
to go to sea.

glorious and white and fluted
sails,
selling up at the metropolis,
and sooting it.

Grim air of salt
and the drunken sea
sliding on its own bottom
(if it got one).

a blue blanket,
everywhere
spray-frayed,
an outing of
coal-holds

cinnamon
the deck-wood
craft calling craft
arm waves ...

till they set away,
this way / that way.

tiny-er

unforetellabler

twistier and distanter

(to the coal-goal)

2

What fire-flags,
all the world's ambition waves, flick-works in time,
the decks an' the mountains an' the jubilant
'Oh trust me, honey …'
cilla (green-beams)
arc-message-energy
and the smooth hand of the sand year …

of the whole reversion to hydrogen,
consider –
well! hell!
if it comes, like
every grain-coal convert to air,
each and release

A matter of faith:
that it all in argument
flare to the fire,
matter by ounce and by parcel
verge into heat – AND
oh! bodhisattvas, 'everything is burning!'
What else can it come to?

chaleur, more, enturn to, the
enthralling glad
and sweat-on, make auburn arm
to bring our heat out, earth-warm.

palm-paradisium, on the beach
scaley-men lounge, snap,
bright turtles sing to, aria-ly, or
high gross of wingsects blur and jangle,
the sun of yore enflames the black back
makes it hurrah and stumble

to write is all fancy
turntable tricks,

and if it all vanishes,
and every word
(to the last syllable ...)
into soundless fire?
(every cent of persuasion
unpronounceable,
nothing motioning the placid drum-face)
no sense makeable.
Mute future.

Yes, the spirals, a dragon,
full purple majesty, de-raised to brickcore
all its fine plate of a thousand years
dis-sembled
(for the same advantages ever first
reared it) – (I mean: it could be completely voluntary)

the whole broken hand
testament of cohesive end,
level and bare,
and the vast-bands done,
and
countless prison dust

and the seeds of matter
the indivisibles,
specks and spiral
turned out to energy, omega,
and the knot is found simply
to go back to LINE.

A lifeless bed of rock
iced and enshadowed /
a tumultuous soup-pool
swerving and burning –
both?

The land girt by dragons,
and the Great dragon,
chained cross-wise at its heart / in the heat.

This I remember
in the warmth of my arm,
in the well-born humidity (water),
and the far-throw of fire.

its unique neat tablets,
stacks of rows of bake-bricks
as each house, the heat in it!

That we should image some intention
wanting to be keeping it together!

*

The advance
to adventure ...

wheelbarrowsful of hi-stepping words
consigned to the pit
to the central darkness
places of collection and disposal

a great in-draught
of energy, leg-bicep / medulla
hand-to-wrist, shoulder-shape,
at balance
with what will be released

the price is
a muddle of
work-content, novelty and demand,
(but in the end, a crackpot one-eared art-man
outstrips the average sea-coal-mine
by fingering the line of supply –
shear & impractical)

and mental fuels too,
it works out
you check your skull-bonnet,
safe-lighting, boots and brakes

before you take to the shaft.

I slot a pie in my pocket
and mash the tea,
hold a cheap biro in my teeth
and swing into the cage.
'How!'

Elohim invokes the engine to turn
and winches it all down
standing of a tray of grips and picks
with the extra rope bobbined round you,
it is all sure down.

here the white-stone and the orange
and the bright black
come all uniformly dull,
and the dead and living march all equally
by lines of cable, track and pipe.

with this art
the props and boards
are recovered with a quick dash
before the roof panics and falls
(goodbye goaf)

or you sideways some good slot
of coal
as far as you can bear it.

And the debris
that fixes in your head by the adits
jams the grand track
till it's shovelled up in tubs,
this quality and that.

Small-coals
and good-round –
look what I've brought yer!
White circle up there, see!

(Aye, but what of the lamp.
Come on, pass me the lamp up, nephew, I'm waiting.)

*

Let us leave by pipe

Show the singing wolves the doorstep
to the day / hymn / thunder,
paint them
the nylon cherry-trees / applause

Never denying it also
it also is

The brittle diamond of the head
there is to shine,
black bone to play pretty

Only there is it sense
and the feeling
and right.

Great grandeur warm sea
mix of movement
a land of petals of potato
and rush-frisk
and tender-bread,
contented.

No speech penetrates;
the born pulse
the home heart
the unGod.

It is sun-froth
and twin,
battle-bread,
contended.

here life-tins,
foot-skin,
rolls and glows,
endued with wish.
It will not consider transient,
not demonstrate non-human,
not know such switches.

the tremendous.

Why should you be spared
disaster?
each arm and face is fuse —
all the present

Engulfed
by the heat
the net of ferns
and
turned to a list
an incomprehension

*

hewer / putter / driver
one biting horse-being
always pleasing

The brakes
bells
and the division dolt
and the love-lock

The slowing seed-fogs
clothe
memorate
revel in granules

Letterboxes
bring me

requests / demands / challenges
greetings / revels

Fish-storms bounce up the beach,
stones, demon-roots
flare and fall,
nose-to-nose fizzy

shoulder-shapes
friends, figures of crab and blood
pray to the new pyx
the black little humance
blown easter-way

the talking nebula
the lift
the response

and the real souls
new-told activators
bring up in great shells
new sounds,
maculations

Let us re-sibilate
see each rib grow
galant

its haze-compass
on the line of

the House-Shaker.
Throws round the world,
ignites
(no, you don't hear it)
turning air into air!

*

The far / fierce

battle-light
replays.
Old worlds
sealing themselves off.

On obverse,
the arm being branch,
scaled chest,
cord-bloom in dark,
deep-bract ear,
elbow, fur,
fern, gland,
and these machines play
bud, seed, soda,
club-jacket,
powder-mound.

Tabby-flower focus:
waist turns to tree-curls, up,
tuners, leaf-top (heads, eyes, hands),
logic of Nature.

It has its ice-house
new authority of cold.
Burden of shadow.

Then
toppled-lighted
patch and wheel, loaded wire-world,
all, end.

In the sea,
each of the thousand fish around
has a track of conscience,
to be forever,
from ever.
So.

Toys, shells,
jerk about,

lemon slice and de-corts
in little spurts of pips.

The regius room, and eating halls
will there be
(let's speculate)
a tress of a spine of a binding
left?

which is longer, then,
thoughts or castles?

Only
time turns itself,
spends in a spread of a blow.

here in the bowl
shines
shows
no.

*

Leper-minds,
leave   it!

Don't mark it, let it make!

From the flying arrow in the day,
the archer, the sun-needle,
from the dark plot,
the doored cell, the concrete, the tunnel,
the inrush
of homelessness,
the demon at midday –   [Ps.91]
will I preserve me?

On the cash-crates
one child or another
sits. Lux.

Dogs tamper with the gutter,
Lettuce and chip-wraps.

Man-growing.
Flip-flip sez the dumper-truck.
And meep-meep.

This time Death doesn't care,
he sends the hotness south,
he stitches the coast into sun-bonnets,
sea-weeds tire into oil,
BELIEVE
in cocoa-palms.

The christian caps his
free limbs,
heaves above the sea,
the skull is muddy and triangular.

For a million times later,
coal.

Trash and hero, baker and pension-prize-winner,
sweet-wife, gin-getter
lucky
to turn up as a frond-print
in an unclaimed
kitchen scuttle.
Benedictus!

While as
the ghoul in the dinery
bellows over his beef and toast.

The savage flares of the yard,
God's dummy fire,
turned up real.

Deliver us from the good!
Say the Book of Violations has shut.

Let us have no more obedience.
Not words, but teeth.

*

The lighted robin
the buzz before the burst

heavy stain of scent
mix-pie into
our fire-nose
the buttered lacquered cup
chilli-mustard
black sunny wallflower
each still-heat rouge-motion fire
what woman can you not imagine comfort in?
– man identify in?
(glaze-blaze at one)

3

Up
the forests
high Canadian mountain-lands
to chug and dawdle
along through

blue crystal sky
tented, protracted tunnels
sun-banana, ice-apple snow,
and many many little empty spaces.

Too:
these
black glinting
mole-way railways
thru tree-lands, phantom-things, mauve
child-shows, redded shales,
shadows of rabbits,
stinks of footways
and oval echo-prints.

pinkish hellish helmet-gear,
friended passing-points,
helps, hand-meets,
over our ground-gaps.
An' a sandwich-packet-hall.
Dark tactless fossil flies
in with fishy feet
and pleated leaves.

Lobster-psalms
turquoise breves
unimaginably for over-head
(part the sand-fronds)
see sense.

A wolf-noose
around the Canon.
He cannot dismiss them,
he does not know the Latin.

This is THEIR
conifer kingdom.

The carbon halo,
hocus-pocus blood-motes,
semp'eternal gristle.
Endless doubtlessness, land-full
surprisedness.

The pole of lorry-hoot
up a lane.
Sudden red letter-boxes.
All the excitable engines.

A funfair day,
when all the rubbed, shiny stones
collect at ridges,
play with bits of boots, slide with dogs,
munch them seaweed.

Slowly, maybe,
but will be told.
A story of thousands of wheels,
millions of spokes,
myriad brakes, axles, whistle-rings.

Hallelujah.
Here you will never hear
of thunder-drops,
mind-slates, purchasements
and small print pixies.

No puzzle
but where
to judge north.

Black is the
abundant salad,
all sunk to coal,
squidged and forgotten
and suddenly
back in the centre of the home.

The God of Sunday
willed it so.

*

I took the seeds
from the coal.
Tiny spittles of fossil,
charming specks of,
(flashing like treasure-boats,
advance adventures),
bedded them
in a loose swamp of soil
to see.

Lucky me.

It thought I had forgot it,
when it all-once slammed up
and crowned
noir-tulip-high.
But we applauded for that
till it blushed
all choc'late.

It masted,
it mated,
it towered.

I never touched it /
thought harm there,
alien-growth,
till storms felled it,

then I made it a boat.

Where is Lucifer's lake
to sail in,
which way finds Tartarus?
Are there tides?

Log-boat,
keep out of the tanker-lanes
nose away the debris,
then give it its head.

Will the classic reptiles swim up?
It holds no trace.
It sings with an old note,
that is all.
It belongs to emptiness now.

Then what is she at?
The boat only wants
to get home.
Demanding no better luck
than harbour-fall.
I acquiesce.
Look at her spin & surge & win.

The harbour-due is three pence.
Their hammers strike the boat.
I dodge the Vulture-One
and go laughing to the pub.

There are no dirges;
the cellar is rounded over with lovely paints,
like a pasta-house.

Some guy with three heads
is crooning a song
about lambs and worms.
Likewise his dog.

We sing.
We play boxes.
Line and weigh our heads on the scales.
Kick up the helmets.

Or
will I be too late
to catch the ferry back?

No.
I row back.

Will my boat be psalms & ferns?

On the live side,
lights twinkle (lick-bright)
and radios sound.

And I have
four
more
seeds.

*

From the cosmic gape,
snow descends.

White day-drifter
settles on every tilt.

It is sharp-smell, acid,
eye-acute, crisp-foot, salutary:
saying
the only route to profit is terror.

Are you cold?
Pay us more for heat.
The *right*price –
The profit price.

(What littlest you can give,
what most you can get.)

Perpetual kidnap.

But only (for you)
snow stability.

With occasionally, a stingy (tart)
snowball round the ear.

Ouch-touch,
nauseate,
lung-clasp (collapse)

Batted
by the paw
of the law.
They're all throwing,
snow-throw – wow!
Like sonic tracks,
arc-and-fume missiles,
the air is full!
A festival of hits, hitting,
missing, boing! pfft!
skeeeeow!

I fear no emma-wheat,
No horse herds me,
sirens & stones & gas are ghosts
that flutter irrationally,
warming the air
with words.
Phantoms, beware!

Knock like linnets
(tick-tack, tick-tack!)
on the cocoanut,
tickle like light.

My stock of snowballs
falls.
I throw anything.
Crunchy globes of news-stuff,
pizza-boxes,
bibles,
now the whole folk
are chucking every thing,
bouncing & crashing & thwat.

Turning the lights on
only
makes it worse.
Targets match.
Bottles & bricks course by air-mail,
down and round,
excited like demon-drummers,
and dogs are frantic, shouting and jumping & catching.

It is the world of white,
where screaming hawks hunt air,
wrappings of snow, paper, fog,
great energies,
then everyone gets sleepy
and stops.

*

Two column-statues
scaleless, coal-built
when-who-knows
why-who-knows
or how.

Old, rounded, humbly,
recognizably,
art, this woman seated,
man standing.

She is level-gazed

(if the rock tells us)
plinth-less but loving
and (if the scatty coal can do it)
smooth, neat-necked,
she as careful as the work.

he is back (recessed),
but taller, as stands,
calm, well-grown, maybe bold,
steadied with hand on her,
balanced so,
but the face worn off
(man, child, puma?)

Sometimes they seem Old Ones
or Youngsters ...
Giants? Carapaces? Dragonfolk?
grand concepts, gifted, formal,
and again intimate, close
(but not open)

I do not bow,
I do not rub,
it is my token of continuing,
maybe it is the house they are in.

perhaps they are night-rulers,
body that copies itself.

I trim the wick in the fridge,
go to meet the second absentee.
Biscuit-children,
water-high-daughters,
who is it I trapped –
a ghost that I saw sight of
inside of a balloon
fretting and shoving.

Take your presents
and see if the couple have moved.

The flesh,
the key to time,
the mobile, hungry, beings of bones,
lipstick-tulips

princely

entire

trumpet-sweet

(and oh)
secret.

*

SERVUS IN LABYRINTHO
MAGNA CUM CAUSA
VERBA TIMET

'The slave in the maze
with good reason
fears words.'

JUSTITIA CUM SEQUATUR
IN OMNEM VIAM,
PLUS ULTRIUS AB CENTRO
PLUS NIGERIOR.

'Though he seek justice
down every tunnel,
the further from the centre he goes,
the darker it gets.'

LIBRA NON SE AEQUARE POSSUNT:
FULCRUM DEEST

'The scales cannot balance
with an absent fulcrum.'

QUOMODO METARE
CORDEM CONTRA PENNAM?

'How can you weigh a heart
against a feather?'

QUID VALET
NISI AURUM?

'Has any substance weight
except gold?'

AUSPICE AURORAM
AMARE FULGARE
TACERE FIERI.

Look at the sun rising
loving shining
unspeaking and becoming

JUSTITIA
QUAE EST FIDES

As if justice
be trust

Metrical Cookery:

A Performance Text for Two Mouths or More

Moretum

There is a shout in the snow
    a shattering sound of bell
And the dark is stopped
    it is a decision to work.
Roughly clothed,
    it reshapes light.
And walks or staggers
    not quite singing
to jingle bells of drink
    dark beans in the hopper
turns and turns
    as the Teacher says
'The Mill is how on-fold worldly-cares
    ever turning round and round the mind.'
And the powder gathered,
    set to percolate,
shakily stirred and sipped,
    in front of the softly prisonned hearth –
what other dawn is there
    if the gods & goddesses of food
receive no honour?

Apple Bakewell

Line a tin with 6oz shortcrust
    spread with jam
and a layer of cooked apple.
    Cream 2oz each butter/sugar
add one egg, almond essence,
    fold in 4oz self-raising flour.
Adjust consistency with milk
    and fill the case so.
Bake 35 minutes, Mk 4.

Apple Cake

Apple Cake:
> *Cream 6oz marge*

is 2lbs cooking apples
> *with 8oz sugar*

cored and peeled
> *then add 4 eggs*

and slice and laid in a tin
> *and fold in 10oz flour*

and covered with this mix.
> *Cook 40 minutes at Mk 5*

then a further 30-40 at Mk 4
> *and dredge with sugar!*

Blancmange (English)

A chilled custard
> *2 tablespoons good*

flavoured at will
> *cornflour, pinch of coffee*

to serve with tinned fruit
> *to 1 pint milk*

or cream
> *mix and boil, then chill*

and be finished for breakfast.

Blancmange (German)

A confection of
> *4 tablespoons*

sculptural density
> *cornflour*

apt to moulding
> *to 1 pint milk*

as rabbits
> *2 tablespoons cocoa*

or any monument
> *mix and boil and set.*

Bramble Jelly

Simmer 2 pints of fresh blackberries
    till the juice runs free.
Strain, and make liquor up to 1 pint.
    Add 12oz warm sugar
Boil rapidly some 8 minutes
    and pot.
It is lucent
    blackly beautiful!

Bread

Bread is body
    and staff
basic
    and rough.
The root of religions
    but never a joke.
Start 1oz fresh yeast in a gill warm water
    to disperse it.
Warm 1lb strong white flour
    (that is stretchy for it to work on)
and ditto wholemeal
    (which is more flavourous)
and mix with a pint or more warmed water
    to make like a thick porridge
with the yeast starter, and set to rise
    where the yeast works on the starch
in the warm
    where it works best
covered with a damp cloth
    to keep it soft
a good half hour
    longer if cooler.
Add in a spoon or two of oil
    for richness
a tablespoon salt
    for taste, though it slows the yeast,
a cup or more oatmeal

for texture
a cup or more rye-flour
    though these are harder on yeast
and seeds like cumin / carraway
    for authentic strength
and knead
    and push and pull and fold and stretch
a good 15 minutes
    to strengthen gluten
till clean and plastic
    and leave to rise a good hour anew.
Beat down,
    knock back by rekneading briefly
shape into loaves and set in a tray
    to prove half an hour.
Bake Mk 8, high up, then 7
    to kill the yeasts and cook
for about 30 minutes
    till resilient, firm, brown, knock-hollow.

Café Au Lait

Richest and warmest
    a mug of milk
of all the coffee-drinks
    a dessertspoon coffee
for morning or evening
    ground medium / coarse
with a match of chocolate
    heated till it scalds
or walnut cake and a banana
    then quick-strained and sugared
to drink and enjoy.

O my coffee-heart,
what an indulge
(what work I've done today too)
with milk – & with honey?
a lovely centre,

tired,
content.

Cake

At dessert
I'm musing the possibility
of a cake in the shape of the Colosseum.
With animals and tigers?
With small choc-lions, wrapped in gold foil!
And Christians too?
Who will eat who?

(Another recipe for the same)

For dessert
a Colosseum
in marzipan
tiny lions wrapped in gold foil and
Christians – should we put wicks in?

Carrots

Carrots can be
    seethe them new in butter with a lid on
cultivated
    or boil and stand
carefully
    in butter, sugar, pepper, nutmeg
most anywhere.
    (And they make a fine sweet steam'd pudding.)

Cheese

Cheeses
    by the grace of God
were created
    to grow the body

and fatten the mind
            on a little biscuit
with beer and salad
            or better, better! much WINE!

They come from Cheshire & Caerphilly,
            from Gloucester & Cheddar,
Wensleydale, Derby,
            Leicestershire & Lancashire (both melt well)
& from Stilton, which you partake of with port.

But if you will know how it is made
            consult the cow:
«My milk make hot (70-100°F)
            curdle (divide)
with rennet or lemon juices
            keep hot, till firm curds form;
next day, cut up the curds,
            strain off the whey
wash the curds
            re-strain
hang up to drain in muslin,
            salt (at 3 teaspoons to the original gallon)
and eat
            or press very dry
coat with melted paraffin wax
            and store cold 3-8 weeks
in your neighbourhood cave.»

Christmas Cake

Module One is
12oz sultanas, ditto currants, ditto raisins,
One lemon, rind & juice, ditto orange,
4oz glacé cherries,
3 tablespoons rum,
to soak overnight.
            Module Two is
            8oz butter, dark sugar ditto,

creamed.
Module Three is
4 eggs, beat & added to
Module Two, then Two to One.
    Module Four is 8oz plain flour,
    stirred into One-Two-Three.
Cook in lined 8" tin,
with centre blocked out, leaving a ring of mixture,
$2^{1}/_{2}$ hours Mk 2.
    Cool, invert,
    daily instil some rum.
(Marzipan is fresh ground almonds
    with the same or less of fine sugar
matched together with egg.)

Chutney (Green Tomato)

Chutney is 3lb green tomatoes
    diced small
a pound cooking apples
    peeled, cored, diced small
a pound and a half onion
    peeled and chopped small
simmered in a pint vinegar one hour
    till soft. Then add:
a teaspoon white pepper
    2oz salt
a teaspoon ground mace
    2oz mustard seeds
a teaspoon cayenne
    some bruised cloves
a bay leaf
    and a pound and a half demerara.
Simmer a further hour and a half
    and bottle.

Citrus Note

'So you're Pip!' he cried
peering over the flap of stone.
I rolled – I gasped
at the sudden flare of the land around:
low walls radiated, a creamy citrus stone,
segmenting the marsh
to neat, soddened fields, gold-flushed
in the sun aslant
over its triangles
wider or slenderer areas of field,
frost-crusted, flat.
So all the rim of the world showed around us,
white, with a low circle of mist.

Cocoa

Cocoa was the luxury
    of the land of new pyramids
and the grave of the lifeboat
    out in the loving waters.
Look, it must be processed,
    the cocoa-butter lifted out,
and sadly still,
    it is indissoluble.

O, Ora pro nobis, Cacao!

Coffee

Coffee looks up.
He sees tall white figures with long high faces
Occasionally, close, an eye
Ever insistent (beat-bar) thrum of
what is their
sing-song bark
some kind / some a nag, they are –
Ladies of sweet and high noses but

The story is allus the same –
Prince of Pearls meets the muck-food.

Curry

Curry is a half pound minced onion, fried golden,
    in 4oz butter
a small tin of tomatoes
    3 cloves garlic (crushed)
1 piece fresh ginger (grated)
    one large teaspoon turmeric
the same coriander
    the same chilli
the same, or less, salt,
    and a cup water
all simmered to a sauce.

    OR:
3oz coriander
    1 of black peppercorns
1 of mustardseed,
    quarter of cumin;
parch in a cool oven
    till crisp
then pound to a powder
    with a tablespoon of Yermesic
and 1oz of ginger.

Diet

Animal products do not combine with each other,
but eat with raw vegetables well;
    Vegetable products do not eat with each other
    but eat with wheat and dairy foods.
Yet the processed (cold/cooked) meats
like sausages and spam and pastes
    all go with processed starches
    (bread, biscuits, pasta)
and vice versa.

Also you should vary
colour
    texture
taste
    but observe the unities of
style
    and culture.

Water
    air
fire
    and earth
should be in each meal.

Food
    complements
work and exercise
    as sleep
complements
    wakefulness.
In a balance.

Egg Poem (Optional)

crew-cutted and stamped
we are all in place
in the egg-box of life

We are 'llowed keep our helmets on
while we're scoured for clap
no-one breaking rank

Or maybe later (shame) we'll all be disbanded
when they find out
who poisoned who.

Never!
Eggs is whiter / brighter
safer / braver!

Then the order comes to get some spotty –
it's all in a day's work
the defence of the defence of democracy

And there is yolk and white
all mixed all over the floor
And we realise, the purpose of eggs is getting smashed.

My buddies and I were jumped right into water
(can Kipling ever lie?)
though it was some shock.

One we saw crash into the pan
All spread and baked up in the heat.
At least we kept our shells on.

For the longer you live, the tougher you get.
The quicker you die
the tougher you eat.

Lamps and lanterns
and caverns and tree-straw were once ours;
all falls to the Great Fork in the sky.

Tremble you eggs!
Wobble you eggs!
Feel the great beauty of the redemptive Egg Mother
    who will fly along one day and save us!

(She is not the pretty ones
we rolled with in the packing shed, but
barrack-talk makes out she is FEATHERED & MOVES!)

No, it makes no sense.
Where
is our oval duty then?

Brothers (you think everything's tyranny), it's nothing.
Some trays are white. Some trays are brown.
Just trust the sorter.

And I tell you
When I hear that Breakfast Bugle
I'm gonna rise and grin, be neat, do my duty, toe the line,
    love the lady,
come up smiling, sunny-side up, and say my thankyou.

Fennel

Fennel is remarkable
    and liquorice-flavoured
boil it
    and watch the water change colour!
It is perfect with —

Fish

Fish you must feed on fresh
    there is no alternative at all.

Ice Cream

This is to be fixed
    four egg whites
in a fierce freezer
    whipped stiff
can only
    and 4oz icing sugar beat in
be kept a week
    then mix in well egg yolks
thaw a little before serving
    and flavouring
quarter hour in main fridge
    strong natural flavours
eat as a summer tea-dish
    and a half pint thick cream
with fruit.

Lamb

Lamb can always be roast
  It serves
gently with rosemary
  as a sacrifice
or a mint sauce
  to stave off the passing Angel.

Marmalade

A bare 2lb of seville orange
  one sweet orange
and a lemon
  put the pips in muslin
in 6 pints water
  with juice, flesh
and sliced peel
  and soak 2 days.
Then simmer 4 hours
  till peel translucent and soft.
Leave overnight
  then remove pips
add more water (to original volume)
  and a pound warm sugar
to each pound-weight of liquor;
  boil 20 minutes.

Meat-Loaf

One pound back bacon, minced,
  the same belly of pork, minced.
10oz fresh breadcrumbs,
  a finely chopped onion
an egg
  a teaspoon dry mustard
same mixed herbs
  some salt and pepper
10 tablespoons cider.

Mk 4 an hour and a half
(cover with foil?)
    Cool.

Meat (To Roast)

To roast, mark 4
    or moderate
for beef and pork
    at 35 minutes a pound
and 35 extra; 30 lamb
    a pound and 30 extra
chicken at 5
    at 20 minutes a pound
and 20 extra, or if
    it weighs more'n 3¹/₂lb
just 20 minutes a pound
    no more.
Roast on the rungs of the oven
    turn each half hour
Cooked when no red seeps out
    but let stand before carving.

Mushrooms

Riddled like a sponge-bone
with air and elements
I float
OK.

Omelette

An omelette is eggs
    beat with a little salt
only improved
    fine herbs or pepper
by a little cream in the mix
    or filled with pre-cooked

or by cooking over wood
tomato/mushroom & folded.

Parsnip

Parsnip is roots
parboil & roast
& like all yellow veg
or fry with a lid
a super
and a bit nutmeg, sugar, pepper
winter vegetable!

Pasta

Pasta is notable
which is boiled
for its manufactured shapes & colours
in copious water
like tubes and strands
with salt
(what tiny, tiny, tiny threads
and oil
the spiders hang on)
till soft
and coloured shells and wheels
(not too soft)
invented by Romans
To make, take
strong flour
or durum wheat (a semolina),
a spoon of oil
and egg to mix,
stand / roll / stand / roll
till translucently thin,
then roll up and ribbon it,
and boil a few minutes
in salt-hot-water.

Peas

Please
    Peas should be podded
also try
    and boiled with a little
pease pudding
    salt, sugar, mint
made with ham-bones.

Pickle, The Pot of

Auburn and ebony
the head reposed
varnished / diamond'
glazed and bottle-nosed.

Vile and green
the head, hot,
flared and stank
with livid spot.

Pink and fresh
the head was smile
sweet with scent
of camomile

blue and boxed
and heart and top
the head's secure
within its pot

or
vile with green
and livid spot

I sing of rose
and jonquil sore
of copper root
in weathered tor

and in the pot
the pickle stops
and pewtered carrots
plip and pop.

Pizza

PIZZA is say one mug strong flour
a bit liquor with yeast and a little pinch
of vitamin C; salt;
a spoon of olive oil and just enough
water to mix, well knead, rise,
shape to a sort of round and top off. (Cook.)

Pork

I find this note:
        'First boil the joint 2 mins. with salt
roast high up in oven Mk 7 a quarter hour
        then on lower rungs Mk 4
about 2 hours or whatever'

Potatoes

The potato comes only
        the potato can be boiled new
from a region of the Andes
        fresh from the ground
and made itself the staple
        or diced, slight-cooked as salad
of Inca civilisation
        w/ a little onion, chive & mayonnaise
as rice raised China
        old ones can be parboiled & roast
and wheat was of Egypt
        in olive oil/butter/marge, Mk 7
where its settled people
        30 mins., turning once or

stored it, piled it,
baked whole and filled or
heaped it, observed it
simply boiled, mashed with pepper
butter milk & egg
and adored it as a
and served as a
PYRAMID
PYRAMID

Rice

An ultimate staple
a cup of rice
of washed rice
to 2¹/₂ cups water
mixed hot with any
salt, simmer 15
chopped sharp vegetable
then stand five.
cold as salad
add chopped pepper
called 'jewel'
of yellow, green, red.
To re-enter
re-heat with yoghourt.

Sacher Torte

A Sacher Torte is
3oz melted butter
a Viennese Chocolate Cake:
and melt in 2oz chocolate
this is quite secret.
on one side. Beat 4 egg whites
fold in a blend
of 3oz sugar and 4 yolks
and fold in 3oz flour
and last the chocolate sauce.

Put in two greased 8" tins
and cook 40 minutes Mk 4.
I forget the rest
(it is improvisatory).

Spinach

Spinach will wash
    and with water adheres
cooks gently down
    then dowse it with pepper
(Only Popeye
    uses tins)

Swede

Swede is fodder food
    dice and boil
and thoroughly good
    mash it orange with butter
for anyone
    pepper and nutmeg

Tea

This applies
    boil water
    warm pot
To any blended
    infuse tea
    in bag or pierced holder
Tea of Indian base
    2 minutes
    remove
Drunk breakfast or afternoon
    as you often are

Tokaj

As golden-eyed
as a pure lemur
I scale the steps to the open air

On the street
on sale are windows
of glossed-black consumables: turn left

In the shop
it is hard not to gloat
it is hard not to play a tune on the bottles

Look at
the vulgar gingery carrot-glint
circling the topaz-sure soul of this liquor

Thus the Romans in certainness
laid their vines, brown-armed,
so long ago, safe to grow, in Magyar dust.

And the taste –
shall I anticipate it?
The pleasing wonder of in-twinkered sun-shiver!

As black-bright
as a Hun-berry on the steppes
I brace my limbs to top the cork – Welcome the King!

Truffles

Ho! they are
as much ounces melted black chocolate
as fluid ounces double cream,
and boil the cream
and turf in the choc
and beat as it cools
and shape
and roll in cocoa.

(This is not the sort
that pigs eat of course.)

Vegetarians

Vegetarians unanimously
reject Transubstantiation –
no divine blood ever warms
their empty tummies,
coffee and salt are seldom on their altars,
no puzzles at all, unomnivorous
attack on unconscious greens.

Viennese Pastry

Cream 4oz marge
    a tablespoon golden syrup
fold 4oz self-raising flour
    1oz cornflour
a drop or two vanilla.
    Bake like little cakes
Mk 5, up to 20 mins.

Xmas Pudding

Make 2 or 3 well ahead
    and they will serve two festivals.
One pound sultanas
    the same, raisins
the same, currants
    the same, castor sugar
the same of suet
    in a bowl;
and a half-pound breadcrumbs
    same, minced mixed peel
and flour
    but a quarter, ground sweet almonds;
2 teaspoons mixed spice

and a little nutmeg and salt.
Mix all and add
    6-8 eggs
a wineglass brandy
    half a gill old ale
to make a thick paste.
    The next day
add another dose of old ale.
    Grease 2 or 3 basins
nearly fill them
    cover with greased paper and cloth
and steam 8 hours
    uncover and cool
fit new paper, cloth, and store.
    Re-steam 2 hours to eat.

Ziziganes

Ziziganes are weeds
    nasturtium flowers
borage flowers
    marigolds (the leaves)
and of young dandelion
    hawthorn
and all sorts …
    You can have
carrots with aniseed,
    peas with basil,
potatoes with poppy seeds,
    tomatoes with basil,
onions with bay,
    mushrooms with tarragon,
turnips with celery-salt,
    cauliflower with paprika,
baked beans with ginger,
    spinach with mace,
sprouts with mustard seed,
    lamb with garlic,
kidneys with carraway,

        chicken with lemon,
ham with cloves,
        pork with dillweed,
rabbit with thyme,
        beef and rosemary,
turkey and saffron strands,
        everywhere
everything is growing
        sun-absorbent hot
and wind-balletic
        and abundant,
self-replicating
        (like out of the hob of the copier
pages come hot and crisp
        not edible yet
but to enjoy)

The Purple Shepherd:

An examination of perfect government
according to the best authorities

1. Aeschylus

The sky was a mad shepherd tearing his own flock;
Ship against ship butted like rutting rams.

'and the people, speaking, in spots
for a purple
shepherd
rao-rao-rao-rao!
– full or small, stiff-eared
limped, scritchy,
scabbed-joint in his teeths.'

The container is shut.

The tea-dust
loose-lets my guts.

I affirm:

There is no paradigm of power
only negativity.

The leader destroys.

The sole dancer,
the exhibition of action,
's the grand block
over oneness

Egregiousness!
So, always,
contempt, tools
of the ladder

More'd, maximised,
compresst, discarded,
(nothing achieved unless)
(and what worth what's achieved?)

More, most,
cuts up the net
that ought to bring together
scats the whole-dance
hate-body
You have boxed the set

tells words what to do
(set
over observation)

walls

For words are the structure of power
each hanging as an order on the lip
each confined to its own vibrant custom
while the sentence-maker will not hurry,
                              need not worry to be concluding ...

2. Socrates

What do we say? Socrates summarises:
Each has his class,   the craft that suits;
some are strict soldiers   dealing sternly in battle
with enemies from outside;   evenly and gently
he copes with his own countrymen,   a caring policing.
Such live communally,   incapable of bribe,
propertyless protectors,   pure of taint.
Children of the people   would be called everyone's,
marriages made   to encourage merit
the young growing   to earn status only.
What more perfect   could be a picture of a city.

Everywhere, elsewhere
cult inanimate:
to multiply into many,
the scrutiny and rejection of organic.
Rock sky.

I see it,
rows in a flower,
circuits, symbols.

star-figures,
cloud-forecasts

everything perceivable
so conduces to:
plays, organises
(is practical)
lets symmetry
make a mark in time

Will I make a gem a horse?
Will I make men geometrical?
Build starfish-control prisons?
Cut eggs octagonal?
No, no call
to manipulate
what is growing already, selfly

Whole-flowers.
Half-fires.
Kitten-prowl.
Hill-mould.

More complex?
More unpredictable.
(less stable in time)

Witches rhyme.

3. Herodotus

Then Periander
sent to the king of Miletus
to find out this secret —
how to govern.
Thrasybulus took them to the corn,
cut at this head and that,
again and again,
till most the field was spoiled.
'That is the art of it.'

And what do we know of God?

The helmet is shiny lacquered hard
(beetle-bone-like)
Wrists break
Ribs crack
And life is nothing (you see) before him.

His decision is every minute/speck of your way,
Your wages, shelter, and who is free to make you homeless.
Sez seriously complaining: expects me to find his car
and he can't even talk proper —
what do they think the law is for — what people?

He has wedged open your mouths with wood.
He smiles: jury-tricked you get this, a cell
or the exit from the city for the flags of your judgment.

There is no contact;
them alone —
keepers of the secret of absurdity.
Only the fool sez in his heart there is no God.

Rather, deep wires run,
every man to immortal …

There they are, talking to their radios

attentive, then an acknowledgement
knowing how to talk to death.

4. Boethius

Why strive (mind-sea-waves)?
Why blame (it hasn't gone right)?
Why not wait (for that death
God shaped for you, bitter enough, that
rushes toward you
flailing with his puppet arms)?
You can see him following-up
every earth-being, bird and beast.
And the fierce hunter tracks down
mankind, never quits trailing
till he secures the prey.
Can't you wait?
(No, we will get ahead of him,
be the beasts that rend each other.)
If you strive so (mind-sea-waves).

This whale of house you know?
are you one with me
know its starts/stairs
artery-galleries?
dark knowledges
(look) make us one
it's fun, all dances
droning and bulling around the yard.

In this tent of skins
this skin of taints,
rebels of laughter
are going to
are going to gain
are going to gain the upper hand

All the winter's

out there
lisped cantankerous ice
to press
to blow
so, so, so

hands habilitate,
backs resist
the omnipressure
and
this bubble of warmth
will satisfy

thickest, heaviest, loveliest,
ignorant of untrust
no, not unspeakable
no, not untruth

And that is it?
The goal of life?
To reach death?

'Animals' say the police
and gob into the crowd.

5. Hopkins

Startle the poor sheep back!
is the shipwrack
then a harvest,
does tempest carry the grain for thee?

And
Do we then kiss God?
or stand mouthing, horses chomping
(before the Maker of winds
and brake-failures,
the Man of Microbes)

as if God made words grandiose
huge as wars (to play reaper),
made of vital-free words
the inexplicable nonsense of God,
sound-colour-pennies into the gold plate,
great dark male pulses
to risk the limits, sanity-abandoned deity –
water-goblin.
Surrenders senseless life to.

But Return of terror
a little skylark that's in, then
all the tightness of the heart
everyone's own verdict of extinction
— who is it this terror?

My shepherd gives me grass and water,
shows me where to go, fends off the dangers,

As the brain of the world decays,
eats itself.

I see a white van,
small square windows,
somewhere transporting,
Why, you are not prisoners but animals.
'Animals!' sez the Priz. Off. Fed. –   [22 May 1990
behold your oven!

Here
lineless
treeless
descentless
factless
potentless
lightless
to die out

Policy, if it is extermination,
Life, if it is retaliation.

6. Nuttall

Both connive at their tacit mutual business
which is world destruction.

a curved eagle
a bathed, brave take
(& cloth-armed, tin, enamel,
plazzy-beaked)
All Austria to U.S.
I see no sign of.

carries itself on,
every riot

hell-of-dog-kink
arm/machine muscle-to-move
bulk of bicep

here cage-leg like broken
in exercise all opens
brave/taught at back.

dark-grass-flail-pole
striped, a procession
mask-of-skull / spear-of-gold

hanging at-high-hands
is to chin-up, I choose;
to float, folded ankles.

to pose the hot springing sun's day
unbanked / blistered
as a blast-tune of horn and sky-warm

knuckle-flute bird
declares / twists / sings
prison's riot's smoke's upping lofty-looking spirals

'hodie vire unmilites
totum carcerem tartari luce
clauserunt / aperuerunt'

how the gloss high-black engine
all carriages / parts
verbs pull.

or dispersed each-leg a-song
ran (own accord) light
a dance sill-souled of-its-work

lime-tremendous the head
centurial no more
disachieved such-its-that-was malice

the fist utile/future
at-play-with-walls passes, improvements,
no hidden-shielded squad in the straight

each cobble with muscle
stone-rain
flying, photo-retreats, rubbish-money

the sinister matchless magic
of curling guts
unwinds, melody-row

sweats the stream
abraids its beat
rubs the royal scent, single-fibre all

dead-butterfly
the broken, slur-mouthed leader
budges in her heather-bricked room.

rings and ears
breasts and femur
all will one day co-ordinate a just body

bone-cap
a pleasure
to be.

North Scenes

Little Scenes

Ice-silences, shake
to sun-gonging quaver,
steaming bright with pansy-purple-yellow
Heimdall at the hi-level bridge
sure on his blue horse
horns
and the curtains apert
on these little scenes.

*

Sweet grey
unbright north-morning
now Newcastle.
All curled,
All diesel-eat
The mysterious rock-maze awake!
I am a rat,
I love it.
And Josh and Rick, Edgar, Tog,
arrive it early
before the platform warms.
Loose-walk, intelligent, knapsack up, out to work,
the steam-dance, to the confident outside.

*

Bit boat on a train.
All the sailor's luggage.
Help. Sit. Drink.
And we'll tell stories
of some new song, some long
affair of love, a new true opportunity.
All the way.

*

There are little legs in the window.
Santa Robin.
Sobbing children drag their parents back to the store
for more.
Well, there is lots of time still to get the beer.
In the great church
the house-of-cards of sound
dares the sea-wind
to pull its ears.
Pubs and clubs are shut.

*

Bland bay roads around
I went
(see the skull of an abbey)
At the smoke side then
Rest out my legs and the river
I longly view
       Broad Soushiels her dark, old face
Me
Set across

(The houses
all turning
like a top part of a time god's hat.)

*

It's a good place, with the Tyne bend
so some kids kick a ball about.
Stakes were all dead ship-building was.
And lass and me came sat
but at the back it's church,
a half-wall makes
Shelter. So. And In this silence,
only the tankers off to the sea
see.

*

A small bulbous bottle
rolls around the bus floor.
On my way and will I like the flat at Southwick?

The lady with the smart suit collar
turns up (to the minute)
to say the key's unlocatable ...

But hey, Wear, away,
the lean years are over,
take it, spread it by sea!

Turn the corner,
inhale, say –
isn't that malt?

*

The sofa-neatness small
polished cell-smell,
passage, stair, chair, arch,
pillar and carpet-tack and beef,
I postulate everything but doors
or windows:
dust-dogs, bands of workers,
money if you tell the truth.
Would you beg in a grave,
move in to live ina coal-mine,
phone in to a police ad, for to get a community award?

*

In the Avenue
of Tiglath-Pilezer
purple orchid-heads, holy roses, rose-bay daffilerbs.
Ancient, sybaritic.
At one window,
a teacher or a wife!
A solicitor's cat ...
And a public figure or public official lives.

They will make love like money
and mix words
and wallop ideas around 'em
at the ears of the little sprouts of the workers
whose ancient cave was black with power
a million-over-years before flower folded and pharaohs.

*

mouse-brown (hair-like) fog
brown-plum (eye-like) fog
soft grains and see-less touch-less
trophies, skulls, customers
come to glint in the moon-shine
at day-loss.

*

Coal-spores clog the sea,
hang like a relish in the air.
They will mend it,
I am coming too,
They will see to it soon.
Why, cherubs,
you anna even ate yor cake.

*

For the sun here is
indubitand
at a diff' angle
& the bronze-knife/rose-flash/sun-shaft
hits slant.

New / same Baal-show

*

First theorem
that the blank angle
the shadow
more blocks, larger.
Such black in day
(where you'd walk)
disquiets.

The second,
for all the sun's brightness,
its coldness.
This is linked to:
the sun swoops by different angles.

And three:
the air's sting.
Not winds' inc.,
but at still, even,
the cold transmission
unanswerable chill.

Four,
the width, blue, clear,
sky-size.
Un-blocked, -screened

*

Little infant
minding a tiny dog
His Mam gi's him a kiss,
goes in the shop.
But now he is dwarfed
by a box of flowers at his back
that gleam for cellophane
each as tall as he
(and like stately columns)

*

So
the whole country from Consett to Billingham is snow.
The dog is coldest, and the small black spider. Only when the heat
leaks from the houses, or comes a constant weight of feet
And all traffic, is there any melting.
Thick ground hands and small ones make snowballs, pelting
People for fun and not for fun till
You almost forget the Quiet and the slate skies (large) still.
And all the dip of Durham is white,
Overnight,
in a sudden worked evangelising
while lads and lasses was slumb'ring.
(Only, to the east lay the sea unfrozen, ships safe in water
And the tugs give a gentle 'Ahooga')

*

It seemed absurd, unapt to talk verse on 'Stanley
Not for want of images
of post-winter fields still patched white and black
packed
between house spaces – I knew –
but for living
(These words wouldn't) just
Want' work in the sun.

*

Dark people and me bleak
At the houses-sides
So I admired.

Don't be sorry.
My anger is a
smoulder-thing, like being blitzed out,
So hot and dirty so we could joke,
a little fire-fount
in my rich blue dark inside.

*

O you gaudy fields
smoked and burned, autumn,
black pattern, chokey, grey, concentric
and cunning gold into
ground-straw-root
and for story-mirror love-blue sky
taste-bound, vast, true
(Thor?)(tight welded away)   [Thornley

Seaham

No
syrinx-van
curved round the bells of the air-wheel.
premium capital in country,
flute-gold-song
every bird and beast an opera.
shower, a volley.

But:
ragwort in a dust-shed
siding in a air-fouled
town,
buddy-still;
bits of glass.

'zigzagged / to the cliff / timid / indoors /
contented into the wet / and noon / came /
skirting and sailing / standing / and handling /
who were / now / but the sea / an unkind /
through the storm-mist / in truth / of the
coast / an ending.'

None of the stones would talk
(a quiet, awesome beach)
at first;
or a tiny one chattered
then a big one mouthed me a hello.
Soon there would be a chorus
of yes's and
also
they shut up some days
(for no reason)
it's a shame.

In The Coal Year

In the hot, the long
summer
the air was marked
with a bilious, flat smell.

Some rammed their
arms
into the cannon
to stop them.

Or said
'they will only fire
water'.

A 1000 goats-without-horns
ran upto the gate
waving their arms against the lorries.

They dodge to the right, the left, the right
Some are knocked flat.

Some made a 'ground-kiss'
Or turn and turn like tops

It is an announcement of drums:
'aux champs! aux champs!'

Even the telephones
are a code.

Work is blockaded from the mines,
coal is blockaded from the steel-worx,
the coal-trains are halted as they go,
the lorries are fired in the haulage yards,
they sit in the pits, block the bridges and towns with cars
and the centres of the dominion are ringed round,
occupied

The great flags
show the helmet and the horseman,
a red sky,
backed with spangles,
fluttring and winding sure
For Sogbo is the protector of flags

In the dark place
between
work-end, work-start, food-work,
in the time of drums
polyrhythmic (for souls)
A THOUSAND YEARS OF COAL

'Aizan! Aizan, hey!
The stupid man ties his horse up
The intelligent sez he will let him go.'

Wash in hot water –
like tents of white and
full of flowers

begging,
a body rubbed with food,
small coins are kept under the ears,
and the necklace is put away
and their possessions
are free from the brutal and chaotic.

How can you come past
the birds on the poles?
the eggs in zigzags?

the eyes are plastered with blue
the boot beats on the tar
the crab and the snake and the helmet

Three-horned-Bosu
with a thin child jutting from his shell,
he

was carried with them into slavery.

To a land
that too shook,
shook, and
the hills steamed, smoked
(it was their own war-time)

Shouting then
(like scoring)
they make march
to the sea-board
skim their corn and flowerpots into the blue
To null the great force of the Ocean:
what will SHE do next?

Moorsrider

Plumstones by the
hotel porch –
It has four pillars.

Are the days, days
of the cornfield
wasted?
Are the bricks of the sea
vacant?
Skelton and Stanghow
are lovely.

Pepper-coated cows
at their grazing
behind furze.

There was
the word CAUTION,
a picture
of a lamb frisking.
Later a
sheep
inside a red triangle,
and the fields were ditched and crossed
and spotted with baby goats
biding meek enough by,
hoofs sliding in
bluey-pink heather bells.

Once
Sixteen Gods
in a violent show-down
smashed up the landscape.
Still the dark bones can
quarrel spectacularly
across the dale.

Six, seven firemen
taking a picnic
there while their larger engine pumped in water,
and rolling about.

Lime people
live here.
Their sheep
are used as milestones.

Who ever thought
of joining the fields up with walls?

The fog has blocked up the valley.
Glaciers were like it once, truly
and ground the land out
thoughtless and thorough,
scooping
(without rime or reason)

The sheep
almost climb in the car-boots
for food.
This is the prairie edge.

Thru the dry streams
I come to the minster.
(It is made for St Gregory)
though he has now died
and indeed anyone else who might have been here.

The minster, Orm's work,
is a muted place,
place of half-worked stone
and plain or missable
ornament.
Tostig figures in the superscript
who killed Orm's father
and
with appropriate guilelessness

he left the names in juxtaposition for ever.

When I walk
there is not much to write about.
Seldom are there any discouraging words.
Excepting landowners'.
But their hearts are cruddier, less cute
by not sharing.

Sweet and taut
this long extending roof of moorland
lies like in a grave sleep:
parts are bracken green
parts, plain dream,
laps and pools of dark-dyed land
folding
at waves and rides

By the driven storm
boxes of Transylvania
come recklessly close.
Probably the lifeboats
bearing deadmen's names
assist them in.

The last landmark
is Wade's stone.
It stands in a farmfield
and the sea and the sun
rising and falling
set and move on either side
as frictionless markers in a meshing cognisation
of perpetual, perultimately largo
melody
composed by Wade, son of Weland.
Good night.

Sixteen Riddles

(for Staithes Lifeboat Day 1983)

1. I fit ina pocket
and when I'm grown up
that is blown up
I'm off to sea
And just see
How speedily
Back.
So name me.

2. Curv-ed and ribbed as the horn of a ram
Almost part of the land
You detach it metallically
Hope it won't shatter suddenly

3. As I walked through a National Park
Awaiting a bus
I saw a giant kettle under Boulby
Steaming and coiling in the damp air coolly.
What is it, tell me.

4. The steepest Z
ended
in like an '&'   [ampersand
stops and sends
rollers thrashing
where the C bends at —

5. Ellerby Ellerby Ellerby round
amazing the maze is that licks overground;
it teases the gulls,
soddens sound,
and hides the houses
so they might never be found

6. (Whitby)
Halfway down the cliff on the 5th February
I spotted a lost tooth
a wise tooth, but it fell, for all that

7. (two adjacent structures)
A monster shape
being part of the sky
as I move its outlines move and change too.
Close enough by
issues some near million-cubic bellowing
at full volume it swole and got swallowed up
(not unbenign maybe the 1000 foot of wolf who could've origined that).
The silhouette though was inactive, bit up or ragged, very grand

8. A supernova of sound!
cliff shakes
foreshore wakes
barrier breaks.
A sky-toy!

9. that spiral up
dozens of tiny peeny tops
damp
and dry
low
and high

10. a cat's cradle with blobs like
balloons, all coloured

11. who opened his eye, shut his eye
sped and went slow also
twisted one way then back again
Admired the scenery very much
liking everything I liked

12. Born long ago
And then hit on the head

13. A king with a snout
a grey-green jacket
a T-shirt white
and a little beard (or barbel).
His fans chase this celebrity far as any
(They much admire
his Good Taste).

14. Some books tell
I fell tooth and tile
1829
into the brine
and I haven't come back.

15. These living are shiftless and parasitic
you could even call them workshy!
Not entirely homeless
but their dwellings crunch thus underfoot, never answering back.

16. La! ic lifode clænlice,   buton lufena ænige;
ġe þa sneocað ond swifað   on stan-naddras ic cierde.

Joanne's Book

for Joanne-Marie Harman

Dedication

The resinous rooms of youth
now shut off: I (have) moved
into larger chambers in the
shell.

Mine
to the product of lovely limestone

Fragme'
mere mode of a whorl
intempestuously
omitted
all too
unnoticed

My great playhouse
of paints and word-makers
who will it fall to?

(To argue
is a word-wrong)

Someone who will sand the whole parrot-house
Re-lift the lubent blinds and air-swings
moist the feather-covered books
& signal full-day.

May you or Paul want it?

The Tempest

Unto these yellow sands
A-yellow shells
Lost, you

Are but a wild-wave (fancy!)
Toppling
Trainless

O You, row-row, snatch-tail
Cry cock cry
For the fur fallen that is on your man back.

And
sandworm, curtsey, kiss,
soft notes – fix tree and
tree

Ceiling floor
join hands
             water and wave

The Toys

Rubber hedgehog – was on its back,
(And) 4 toy feet – they were in the air.
All the toys were worth looking at.
Tortoise! Duck!
That solid though, white but
And blue and patches. And up, the head.
The duck pink/blue like for a song
It was I tell you, plastically, winged, for singing.
So the bee:
Buzzaya, buzzaya, bulla, bulla
share money …

The lion was a law
beautiful, brotherly.
And the wool girl
One and one and one.
If you are not famous.

Ely

Winter Ely
In cold street run
I got a blue exhaust mouth
(Was lost wind and the fire off the towers)
Little brother you're cold, my girl friend is;
This warm sound
Pleasing as fizzing and a record round.
This nut this bolt.
Not me, you.

St Albans

The birds, blue backs, watching
The seasons
Detailedly
Flutt'ring (the trains, the raucous scale)
By the window, by the teapot
The dried apricots
On a sun-plate
Form
themselves
Into a yellow pattern.

In Yorkshire: Mark's Slide

Arriving at Arkengarthfell
  a play so perfect
    rose sun on taller parts
      opposite, the sheer stone rounds
        of the hills' ridge
          wildened to redcurrant
            over the ruin-sheds
              Mark would like to live in
                and the concept of it
                grew its snail round and round
                to the full.

Joanne-Marie's Swimming Manual

CHAPTER ONE: HOW TO UNDRESS

For your ticket you take one of the wire carriers and put your
clothes in it
socks to shoes
coat for frame

The trick (being bigger) is not to pack so well as to forget your watch
Now you will be ready

It is possible to buy tiny animal moulds
normally for jellies
instructions
for marzipan carrots

even the apple is food but seed
and a symbol for sower: and as shiny as silver

like a white ball:
plastic: played about
quick as think-it in
ball-boot
stone-bed

glass a bottle
tinkling in and out clean
some jars
sparkle all

four-three-two-one
a skip ana skid and around around around

CHAPTER TWO: HOW TO FLOAT

Racing against Red Injuns 1840
Side-stroke 1850
Front-crawl 1870
Gliding underwater 1880
Back-stroke 1900
Butterfly 1930

it is like a furnace of water
a shiny fire
whipping the curls upward

or stay quite straight (ears lower for that)
like being in a mirror
(mobile)

to begin with, make a series of pushes
push hand: push foot
observed by watersnails
with their slammed chests
slim variegating bruises
arrogant hissing
and brocaded jerks

not freezing or fighting
dancing or moving is floating
and speedless

omit the nose

the breath-coördinates are the stroke
mustard, rape and ice-green wheat
called winning-in-water and working-in-water
heart-save and harmless

meanwhile's
a warm afternoon
staying with me at work
like a long roof round

sometimes

to stay in very long you need more clothing

CHAPTER THREE: WHAT TO DO AFTERWARDS

wash well

save something

like: a warm winter jackal atrot
ears popping

they mayn't seem necessarily the same clothes
but they are.
Christ! they will fit you

there are swings
a little up the road are three chip-shops
tomato sandwiches
or a little nap maybe

shake and fret the hair
air the towel

APPENDIX A: LONG-DISTANCE SWIMMING

a bright yellow a scent
a new thing: a decent joke
nantem aquatilis praeripiens bestia morsu momordit
saevissimo!

in estuaries
a swan paddles
framed w'sand-castles when it's raining

APPENDIX B: SEA-BATHING

stepping on
stones
sweeter is gravel: funnier than mud
a bumpy bar of chocolate in the sun

in the heatless time: holm storme wēōl
won wiþ winde: and winter fixed tight the waves
in an icy grip

APPENDIX C: DEEP-SEA DIVING

mire monoxide, lethal and mental too many, admonished. In air cylinders, the shape of a spoon or a sand-dune, or a tree or a crystal, breaks and branches and is enbulbed, from the cranial sockets like shiny new-grown candles, symmetrical and silvered-on, revolving, distributes stripes, that rainbow, or magnesi-lights, blue Zions of them; red changes to blue, photoing and festooning wrecks, humourlessness, in the senses, no difference in light intensities indicate the surface, tangibly, bubbles do if visible, look for some object, misplaced like as not, pearls are luminous patches overhead caused by the sun, tra'lucent on screen. All diving outings should have a leader, the dive leader is (of course) responsible to the expedition leader, the job of the leader is to loot the site, to be admired, to employ ire to outwit and weigh pressure, the mire ... (repeat as)

APPENDIX D: SYNCHRONIZED SWIMMING

alyssum makes ovals
poppy-round are apples
the spin is geocentric
the lily zigs
dire blue the vetches gyrate
double-tomato figures of eight
Borage feeds itself
seeds itself

loves the bees
sprawl as it please'

A first swimming-pool was opened in 1828
The average pool with people is
probably intended to be synchronized borage

the grape rolls
the seedling somersaults, fly-plummeting
the circle marigolds, and with folded spotted wings

Aluminium
the scent of it!
like in scrolls of spinach, and pawing horses

For the little one:
at the seaside I saw a silver shell
By the water I heard a little bell.

CONCLUSION: ON SUCCEEDING (APPROXIMATELY)

Running about thru the water
What is like
the
never going down
into the pit?
not a
let us go down into the pit

A boulder of gold
for a door-stop

In the mornings you wouldn't know me from Adam he says
She looks back: and what the hell for have *you* been and bought skis?

Family Spell

Self:
I am a person
I keep my keys in my pocket
I bought a second-hand wallet at a jumble-sale

Alf:
deep-black low
ocean drummer
to white
duck-water

Pauline:
sideless play / player
unwon battleplaces
bright sweet metal pieces

Steven:
a gibbering
pint-high puppet,
bones, legs, punches.
Maybe he's c'rect enuf
making everyone at odds.
no one exorcises.

Tina:
Beyond the princess:
gulf as great gap
between horses horses, race-horses, any horses
and clocks or flowers or paints

Paul:
tinker
train-driver
boxer
soljer
stands and thinks all day
of trust

and friendly countries

Joanne:
by the day
she most needs comfort
at night
her spells of sleepiness
spring round the house, make it quiet

Floyd:
he sleeps and chases and runs
and makes gentle objections
but never there's trouble or nothing like sterility
while

Thumper:
hardly counts
properly even, yet; listen.
The two try out
some hymns
sometimes.

The Two Ducks:
If they were witches
with miseries and fires
some love would still work through
urgent with great teams of jaguars and lynxes.

Midnight Scene with Cousins

Let us go downstairs!
(Danny? Angela?)
Shh! I heard something –
(What do you want? What are you after?)
We had better go upstairs!
(Alright, just one biscuit)
What about the chocolate ones?
(Your Dad woofed them all last night)
No he didn't.
(Yes he did, I was looking for one myself)
OK, ta.
(Cheerio)
Oops, my bixit's rolled downstairs ...

Handling Rodney

laurel, privet,
oil-plant, ivy,
horse, keep past.
He's spooked.
His horn-foot hips up the air,
the eye has took bird in,
I am sprawled
aside.
Well, eat grass then,
too much!
oats and apple – enjoy.
*(Aye, in the Catalogue
you pass for men.)*

By the Wye

the slice'flour'tange'-yellow
in about/against the undergrowth green
So my sudden son
made known & 'swritten.

kit-opal
grace-crazy
veins illuded

least-measure cat
guiltily stealing child-available bed-space
the pushover / less welcome

1000s on 1000s on 1000s of Wye-pebbles
(O-pebbles)
dry now on shale-straight

Riddle with Goatsbeard

Golden all-open
all-O
golden clocks,
gilded arms
brave unclosed
air-height (A)
all-gold in umbrellas
vanes, air-leases,
parachutes
open and all,
a windmill, a seed, a girl, a sun, a day.

At the Junction with the Slough Arm

At the start
(why not at the start –
THIS IS
Rabbits
(Ip-yip
peril-coral ears,
bo-younce
& woody tail-tubs)
you could have
from the curtness of the sward
guesst it,
I suppose)
I?
Half-night still
sultan's story-pause
the throat –
murk-straw and the
logs in rot and
these are all dance-live,
stink-tufts
body to body
greasy-padded …
No, a little joy,
lap-legged wall-rail; hatted spirits
pursuing sun-tunnels
over balances and beams.
Limping.

Mark's Poster of Wales

Or Wales –
high
green-rocked
bearing auriferous tourists
to deep (cold Satan's tomb) valleys,

lush-wet
then dull, empty mile-baths;
tiny roads
over ever-growing coal
everasmuch grazed on
underground
Riches or rain?

In The Car

cut gold
burnished gorse
headlited then gone

understars
that is cats-eyes on the stark
consistent black

baking nightlights
branded out on the road
soundsigns

each syllable
slotted in
a bell to chime

Charm

By the corner of the biscuit-tin,
By the plant half-pott'
Lace-cloth / sand-picture / clay-frog
I would invoke
this
minor
love-charm

(Alan & Joanne).
If words are hearts,
mixes make,
knots acknowledge and acquaint time,
then I suggest
you make up / be possible
(Alan & Joanne)
Becos I had forgot
how well it works.
Silent & Taut, Active & Yeast-Thought
as share
slip to
declare.

Proem

On your key-ring
Your gap-toothed, sprawl-smiled photo of
Who is missing

(I used to call him the three-letter-one
to avoid upset)

It is not meant aginst you,
Alf's absence.
He is playing with something
somewhere in the world ...

I mean,
Would you be a radio
and keep yourself in a box?

This boring pub.
Boring Steve.
Paucitous mind.

One Hundred Images of a Captured Friend

1. a sunny lamp
on a table

2. an egg
rolling about in a
cardboard box

3. chairs of oak
moving on a floor

4. some hidden ice
in cold coffee

5. skeins of raw wool
tending from a peg

6. five or six
tinted buttons

7. a handful of
dandelion

8. looks at
the machine-loud
laughing children, calls them
woodentops

9. a black Dane
stalking the land

10. a doubtful or leaning ladder

11. berserk dog
in public

12. a
dismantled

motorbike
carefully piled up

13. a magpie gleefully
hiding a
blue wing-bar

14. sandwiches

15. changes of scent
at tide-turn,
the change of scent
at tide-turn
to new

16. books like
Natural Wonders of the World
Douanier Rousseau
The Ascent of Man
Treasures of Tutankhamen and
Grimm's Maerchen

17. a sparrow tied
on to a arrow

18. a name
wiped off the blackboard
before anyone can see

19. spider-toucher

20. having
some sort of
name or plot
running
right thru

21. a neatly folded
jumper

22. dice that
roll to pairs

23. the one
that walks at night,
a whistling

24. bottle-opener

25. the one who
waits up for pre-dawn
when Thor and the
Wanderer, the elderly one,
can be seen snatching their prizes
before any sun is showing

26. the spark
that sets up a haystack,
un-musical matches

27. marshaller of large dogs

28. a baked brick
or doubled tile;
everyone will be re-incarnated as house-brix

29. impatience
of a quick car
not quite a plane

30. a small river
with boats, dumps
and trucks turning out

31. jugs
that tell jokes

32. fated
to make parsley
for fish-windows

33. the satire
of a herd of horses
in a rich desert

34. a hill-path
and
unnoticed Egypt

35. a rude beast
with no cave

36. eelruse and
eel-pot

37. a crumpled sheet of instructions

38. a bush of Ribena

39. six fish
fighting their way
into a vivarium

40. subtlety / caution

41. a host of
golden
subtlety
– a show

42. a self-assessing
answerer

43. a chieftain's tent-flag

44. the evaporation of orange halves

45. a mace
also turmeric

46. *lustbarker* — merrymaker and
lionbender — liontamer and
kotschuetzer — young soljer and
rolo — a grudge and
seawoof — jetsam and
pow! — a peacock and
fruitknob — bud and
foxburp — red beard and
retchfussy — furry-toed

47. grand
dive without waterwings

48. a quartzite
engine

49. no one
taking

50. the howling
of trains
not properly looked after

51. the sleep
of TV

52. a suggested west front
like Crowland

53. a gang
of cheery up-earwigs

54. the grave
of Hamilcar

55. a rehandled fork

56. the slow grind of
procession, the
street-ghosts

57. sloping showers
in fox-land

58. streamy,
striped

59. somewhere,
a dull
falling
star

60. ebony
directories

61. a non-prince

62. cornet and
catapult

63. empty feet

64. church of
rough rock
in the
crack gorge
of the
limey stone
or chine

65. a slit
tomato

66. hewing
firewood
laying
great fires

67. the festival
circus

68. the
ball-shot
shoulder

69. cymbals
or departure

70. rabbit,
foot
in wolf-mouth

71. an
unplanned-for
skyline

72. fastness

73. no-hope
patrol

74. a bar of runes

75. at the galaxy
periphery

76. odds quoted
on dying

77. flattened straw
strengthened ice

78. the
train
start

79. sins
luckily self-forgiven

80. a fusee
or flare

81. gulp
yearn
wish

82. accuser
of half-heroes

83. a dot
or centre

84. all the thrust of the legs
the spread of both hands
as twisting shields

85. fending talons and beaks
a flight of eagles

86. after the ride of the Khan's horsemen
the cliff-leap comes

87. blind to nothing

88. in the straight dark
with the banged head
look at the loss of sense

89. that jacket
knotting with snakes

90. about talkless terror –
and who makes it?
and the diner and the slaughterer

91. co-operation

92. urgent distrust,
segregation

93. the social acceptability
of imperfect information
being smiles

94. look at
main aim
only aim

95. once the Idises settled here: sat in this spot and that
some chained the enemy: some tied the captains
some unclinked: the handcuffs of the friend;
unspring the locks!   let no one tell of it

96. Weland sought
the material for wings
his swans to clammy cells

97. towing
to sea

98. attain

99. the bustling fruit
of a new settlement

100. the high tone
of the motor
(that works)

Now
By this safest room
most privately doored
boxes of associations, memory – be paused,
in spaces faintly planned
deposed.
Associated boxes, and mind.
Sort them, and decide,
being sixteen.

Other Poems

Prince Igor

Overture

Breath
pale furs of sweet, speckled flower-eaters
displayed
gauged
but in a slow light
of day-print
energy
teases to
is drawn to such sliding lengths
the buzz ova lung
a beatitude

Prolog

A pre-grim station
a plaque
fails, does not assuage
voices of coffee-laden mountaineers
jibe at the sure vows
on stage
there is indication
of eclipse
under-line
there is bears
not basses
cheer if you can

By the river
traitors salvage the ice
& look to store
the notes of sound
exactly like swallowed milk.
Others keener.

The Prince of AD 1185
sets off against the Polovtsi ...

Act I scene 1

Trapped
lucky tinkling
proceeds as a pot of drink
a counting song
a game of song
not so the servers
discounted
in a new state ...

the ice-rakers
remember ingot-making
their patrons
come round wheel-like
like the dancers of bright boots
pushed frontwards
forwards more & more

Act I scene 2

but
Yaroslavna celebrates
a slow recapitulation
of the parted Igor
balanced in wonder
cadence
self
casting for the present
down runs the thought
a foreboding
taught by instruments
interdicted
disturbed
with the stealings of state

never soon righted
now let the pace of bones
& horns
prepare the tide
of stories
defeat ... resolve
tolling alike
a heavy, heavy bell
before the Tartars.

Act II

Inside the camp
('solarised ... psychedelic')
the prisoners are margined
in voice
in tramp
fraternizing even
so clear & fresh
the care of these strange friends
more Russian than Russia
it is after the first dance
that the full spread of their concern
the breath makes note
before back-skirl
then loves or a lure
undefined yet
this now is Igor
does
& with swinging strength
establishes what is absent
or the Christian weights or some blackened, cherished book
of clashes
in the very lintel of this venusberg.
that is Konchak Khan, I think
of lush world
souls of curl
& lap-leopard
hopeful in coalition

listen to the thin bar-
baric winding of tune
looms of feel now
that repass
repass
full & gentle
or zag in man-pulse
open the hill
shape the great halls
horse-dromes
song
beat & beat
round splendour
or sword-dance
lynx & kite
charge
they leap & sweep along
that own the music
sometimes hard of line or plain of joy
but move & speed
who cannot join
hear

Act III

ignominy
antipathy
the over-balance of foes
or the stark strings
work
Igor will depart
will be West
setting the escape.

only Vladimir will achieve the union
a divergence
though
an alarm

and tribute.
short (so left 1890).

Act IV

To the beginning
to the home of Yaroslavna
tense with desolation
the solo of the land
in unattended trust
watching
the slow silver
far lines
with like half a hymn
points of ruin
relaxed
to a new horse-print
the repeating or cantering
of return
for Igor
what gentle
readmission & telling
for a stronger future
where the ice-rakers
catch themselves as fools
trip in a dance
they will be bleached
with the grinding of return
nothing happy
but as a bell
sign themselves into the news
which is also a joy
a song
a thanks
a round of jerking sound
or solemn.

Songs (after Schubert)

It snows.
Did it blind me
to her unapproachable status?

I am the wind's then.
She is th'roughly
A rich bride, for elsewhere.

The first
foot of winter
treads at me, my eyes!

All its tracks of ground
loop and lean
around me

The dustless curtain of leaves
the balance of threads and lines
blows away

Backward so as
highroads
cannot lead.

But there is a slow march
of water
removing and moving

Would there
be any (any marsh rose?) anything yet
to look at?

Lone and grow
these ravines (straight-topped)
such sparse stone.

Like the upset of winter.
The stolid, insistent
Turn.

So let the turf dance
before the dull clawed
dawn!

So blue,
So blue,
So white.

Look!
I look for letters
as though they could cross over.

What a mockery at me!
The man who is weather
falls from recognition.

The company of the crow,
an unconsoling
patter of hands.

The sights of one age –
They do not rise
As they move.

The gateways of land
crammed with dogs
and the rattle of their shutters.

The brisk spout
has its own counter –
For they switch back to back in winter.

Steadily lost
in the cross-working
ways, yet all the impulse.

As unmistakable
as
a bear.

In Dumb Town
the pacing memorials
will not make room.

What more
than the reckless janking tunes of this open world
if I see myself.

This extra puzzle.
Last and full
with new-laid options.

Vanishing perfectly
into
each other.

Short Bestiary

1. The wind rushes past.
In this weather
the dog can't catch bees.

2. In the garden next door
a woman
clapping and clapping with her hands
to shoo off a magpie;
in case it steals her mind.

3. Here the wild dog
sniffs first of all at the boots
sometimes stands up at you
high as he likes
or even lets you pick him up
as he licks your face.
It is my image for fire
in the land without company.

4. A rainbow?
no, a loyal royal baby.
Is it a Saxe-Coburg do you think or more of a Battenburg?

5. The Parliament of flowers
does not permit exclusion.
After one, or two, or three
hundred years
then a full meadow
can likely be looked at.
What do you think?

6. When I was no older than –
when I had had a good bit to sup and
when I was climbing into –
There was a sound like someone picking away a lock
tapping, tackling away outside.
Just a bit unsteady then

I put an eye to the glass (having thought it over): look a
hedgehog was there, and an empty dish
of foil in its teeth going
bang bang bang bang bang with it because of
parading up and down for milk.
Not silly at all, that one.
(I called it Lee)

7. I have an arrowhead
it will swing at my neck
I will dream of hunting
– like a bright hour, all wordless
– running and eating
till all the morning animals wake me up
and ask to be friends again.
When I woke there were two coming to the bed I had left.
And when I wait for bed my face is greasy with the heat.
But think of somewhere everything is easy to do
tho you need the energy.
Imagine being a mechanic.

Second Family Spell, Without Names

A world of self-facsimiles,
like motives and meanings.
professional people
can show it is the material
that is flawed and degraded.
Some are just units for looking at.
But to be visible.

Around
as a world funfair
or roundabout.
not going.
People stand about
kick their heels
till it starts up.

Smooth paste stones
arranged as marmalade
sneer to silly to excited to fierce
to sneer again.
If she will set or settle.

The gentle rebellion.
as if wheat or milk
while wheels and seagulls
see their safe eggs
launched and changed.

For the little one:
at the seaside I saw a silver shell
By the water I heard a little bell.

And when the Princess Tina would not laugh, her parents put an
advert in the local shop, said 'Anyone who can make the Princess Tina
laugh will be rewarded with her hand in marriage'. And do you know
what? No one answered the ad at all.

Weight-Training

Today too my weight stands
under 13 stone
but I cannot yet lift an equal.

Out there the sky has been grey
after several fine days.

The weight of the whole building
above this small bright room
is incalculable.

The start is to warm up,
that is to set the rate of heart and keep it.

At each end of the bar
I set over 30 pounds
from hip to chest raised and lowered straight

between sets I don't pause
more than 10 breaths.

The second are curls
the arms very straight at bottom
flexed quite closed at top.

This is done
without jerking or bringing in the back.

The third is to raise the bar
well above the head
from shoulders till arm-lock at top.

A belt drawn tight on your waist
keeps the lower back steady.

The first round is five
the second six each and so by increment

to ten repeats.
I exhale at the stroke of more stress
inhale when the stress's less.

At the end of the second round
the heart rate is high enough to keep working,
the pause enough just to regulate it.

the scent of the pool comes this far.
I use the corridor for more air.

the grip is shoulder-width or more.
Each action uses both strokes of the exercise smoothly,
isolating that one or set of muscles.

neither snatching up
nor just letting fall.

At the longer set
I take 3 sharp breaths before,
three after, extra.

And in the pause
keep the muscles moving, rehearsing

Sometimes untying the previous way,
or flexing for the next –
uniting the whole.

Not stiff but supple
as you do more, and take more.

The concentration is with it
as loose as the muscles
as close as the continuity

No outside images
seem to play here

But like the night action

of a full flower
close to the space of the centre

the thought feeling to the muscle
the muscle being the thinking

In 30 minutes or more, the
first round of sets is done and when
it's easier still I'll increase weight.

In doing
I am growing

I set the weight at 220
it is machine with a bar that travels up
as you extend your legs, back against ground.

After an exercise with head low
it's worth a little pause before getting up.

In the second of these
lying on a bench
I set forehead to meet knees – crunches.

Exhaling
as the stomach contracts.

Another, with an overhead bar,
I pull me up and let down
– my whole weight

But as yet only one, two or three
each time. Pull-ups.

In the 2nd set of crunches
left elbow goes to right knee
right elbow – left knee.

Because the muscles of the stomach knit
by varying the exercise

With the leg-pushes
I breathe when it's at top,
also stretching my toes up and down then.

I increase it 5 thro to 10
and not bouncing the bar off the springs at the bottom.

With the others, as many as I can
my limit
is what I repeat each session.

That is 3 times a week
or once each three days.

For I amn't efficient
but practical
that is aim beneficial

So my health levels
so my body trims and broadens in power.

For work only part works you,
and the punishments set leave you
like the devils who make them

here in this you can live
like alive

By breathing
without coercion
without misoperation

A stream not intent
to go uphill

And sit-ups
done free with back off bench
or at an incline

and twisting
side to opposite side

developing,
the sun shining and shining brighter
but never seen to go back

I have reached a point of half-way of
Ninety minutes

With the belt looped round the bench for my toes
I've done inclines
now it's bench-presses

They are more than all the others:
as dragons to hawks, or orange to white ...

The Great Cheese Fair

Of Norwich in 1815 I have a story to tell
Of how the Great Cheese Fair did not go too well.
The price of cheese was so unfairly great
The people declared it was wrong to sell at that rate.

They seized all the cheese they could find on the hill
Set them on edge and sent them rolling pell-mell.
Down all the road-ways the cheeses rolled straight
Such a ripe cascade of foods it would be hard to beat.

Then the mayor rushed out this riot to quell
And found the lanes bouncing with cheeses of ripe and full smell.
A couple of choice ones knocked him off his feet,
And dozens and dozens more rolled on over him in the street.

Grief that the Palestinians are Treated like a Tribe of Onions

(18.9.82, after Exeter Book Riddle 65)

I am ALIVE
I SAY nothing, still
I am DANGEROUS.
BEFORE I was,
I was BACK.
EVERYONE robs me,
KEEPS me in CONFINEMENT
and shears my HEAD;
CUTS at my BARE back,
TWISTS my spine.
I bite
no MAN
unless he bites ME.
There are MANY
that bite ME.
First the WARRIORS
were sent AWAY,
but it was ONLY a RUSE,
to EAT us all up.

Two Summer Poems

Up on top for all of all famous Wednesdays woz a growling moor
While prince ministers transmute 'emselves entirely to godhead
        informing us they are puzzled, angry, worried, resolute, by
        turns; metals like red and green are very pleasing here

Boiling moss of gold-chrome and tin-green,
        just a fence changes it to pasture before Freebrough …
It is surprising after how few miles you can see the sea
    Quite high up even insidemost the dark shire

(Danby Low Moor)

While the pigs were at the palace trough
    Battled I with dotted red lines in Loftus Woods
A grim and grotesque procession thru the hogweed.
In Enid Blyton, now, of a sudden '*Castle, remains of*' would have
        bestridden the path

    'Funny' we would have said, consulting the map – with an adult
    frown –

'Kilton should be another mile down the stream!'
But our only mystery was the way out and what sort of a timetable
        was operating at Carlin How.

(The Kilton Valley)

The GLC Abolished

Time to wake up again. The usual bears at the window. Could the daylight too be growing?

A solemn morning.
The monster goats
stir, in the out-fields.

And in the day again
Past the window, warm, and in
the light plant-down shifts and stirs.

I am thinking of small things as I take breakfast, like any other day. Suddenly to stop. As tho I had forgotten why I should be uneasy. Or what sorts of foolery are afoot, with the smell of discord.

On the hills
the wolves and foxes lie down and discuss
what more the government can possibly do for them

It is as tho something is taken away from you, and the thief returns to punish you for carelessly losing it. What can you say? Yet there is something more than just grotesque about this day; it is self-defeating:

The mouth of the dragon
twists
to bite its own tail.

For today, the government will make a city disappear. No more London, not even a shire to take its place! I open the windows of my friends' flat to watch the transformation, uncertain what is happening.

Exhilarating?
over the plants,
the mountain range.

In the width of windows
viewing the warm brick
the sides of the mountains.

There the houses
are folded and waved

in a complex of mountains.

The wall that is faces of houses
is plain and square: such brick
in new mountain-building.

Curves keystoned,
brick arches in roman threes
like mountains, ancient, again.

present as a curtain wall
that are cliffs
and ridges

And at night
the lights are here then there
in the caves of the face.

The Uxbridge Workers

Invisible demolition
as near as
transparent

Ordinary jeans
a back, brick-coloured
rough, dusted fingers.

Head at work
hair turning to cement
in ridges

Or
no clothes much
but just jeans, blue thru to the sky.

Rosy-shirted
grinning
and brickpink at throat

A glazier
unsouled almost
how it bounces off his eyes.

Bright tattoos
of snakes and ladders
climbs up

One, singing at the top
unnoticed
is a crazy thrush

And lifting
broad in a block
shoulders wood-sharp

Balancing
on a vault of legs
on a curved plank

White vest
cloth-chested
glossy to paint in

Like with pulleys
topples
leaps

And a scaffolder
growing out
in new tools

Signs of ruby and blue
in the shake-wet of the head
and sun.

Two, three, more
a rainbow
mobile in line.

Arms bare.
like rods
assessing the run of the wire

A whole frame of lines
standing, stretching
on the parapet

Lifting-up
high over wavy ribs
chisel-stuff

Taut-backed, his dance of looking
as every girl comes by,
attentive like a goat

And one guy
with a trowel
nursing skulls

Over a slab-sea
lapping
at the foot of the towers
seeing the sea-bed.

Serious steel
on station,
Not gunned but guards though.

Untitled Poem for 4 Voices

1	2	3	4
On the seaward wall	on the stone, on the walkway	the slow watch	the waiting, the reworking
At the placid clouds	Over the float, so long forward	At the climber sun	Flicking pencils at the waves
First the emerald	The eye, moon- stone	And the diamond	Fourth, the amethyst
growing in green	tricked in true light	frozen, the target of fright	bruising, brisk, browning
Each a token	A tower on the boat	Each taking its place	present in the tale
And the grave warrior	And the lovely queen	quaint, unique	in the hand-made world
Each tide bringing strangeness	bone from the desert	drums from the other continent	scouring the circum- scribed world
waxes and brash dyes	bluings, mordents, helterskelters	pretty, hand- woven treasures	new fruit, sweet & proving
small, traded fragments	lessons to new lips	tipped with red spice	protracted un- certainty

instruments
to
measure

factors in
stubborn
demolition

standards
of
heresy

the ship
turns

the
absorptions
of a new
branch

an
evolution
of town-
ship

quick!
at the
tiller

the guardians
of the coast
turn her back

unable

sad with
decision

not
without
puzzle-
ment

as tho' you
can choose
tradition

At Matlock

1

steep
friend-
  shouldered
    hills

the
solemn
Abraham

hunt-
conscious

the foot
matches

  a
frailty

  ass-
and
spire-
winged

a tawdry
  blow

if sight,
alone, is
not enough
  success

2

the
morning
  from the
    car

the
  victor-
folded
  land

the grace,
the glow,
early
  day

near the
utmost
  path

glazed,
  dented

dire in
the hill

in the grip
  of the
    claw

cannot be
kept,
and felt

3

walk up,
walk up!

the mazed
paths at
either
  hill

in a party,
  all the
    trees

a clove
of
fluorspar

soughing
  apart

long
and blue
fire

ground's
glass

cannot be
left, *and*
shared

4

the very
heights
of the
heptateuch

sloping
at
  either
    hand

sometimes
loose-foot,
sometimes
a panorama

a
  finding
amethyst

a glance
  of mind

the
  phoenix

lovely
  mauve

touch, too,
marks the
rough gem
of spar

Exposition

1

The plunge
of the
paddle-loop

There are
red, cocoa-
coloured
leaves

The sip
into blue

What are
the beasts?

dust
and
dismissal

past
matadors

These are
the places
of action

If I am
slow

2

The back
and swerv-
ing bird

twisted
in
ropes

the gem,
spectrum-
special

The pluck-
coat raven
& the eagle

the tassellated
vertebrates

all the chapters
of energy

of extra
dimensions

a witch of
steadiness

3

These are
the hills

I swop
them
round

sometimes
jackal-
dark

And the
wolf,
wild-
smile

like tall
clothes
of death

claims
of in-
evitability

patted
new
planes

a virtual
scarab

4

The clacking,
ferrous
lines

they are
long, long
branch-roads

blazing
like bikes
and stags

The birds
at the
bank

more than
ever
in I am

why
good-
natured?

bursts of
sun-show

slower in
the world

The Long Barrow

for Keith & Sarah

1	2	3	4

There are
  stones,
simple &
  large
	A standing
	place,
	long-long
		A list of
		  static
		embellish-
		  ments
			Loose lengths
			  halted &
			held
			  in rows

Over the paths
there is an old
  pattern of
  fields
	the frozen
	  pinch of
	  old owners
		open air
		and shut
		enclosure
			the clock
			tips & turns
			in pasture

Speedwell
here.
Loosestrife
& Traveller's
  Joy
	their tops
	  in
	the sun
		the resting
		  point in
		  the
		  growing
			the breaks
			& umbrellas
			of the
			  flower-heads

a glaze of
  stern
  rain
	a church-like
	blowing &
	  tumbling
		chattering
		  surface
		  water,
		  chosen,
		repeated
		  cadences
			humming &
			whishing down,
			  a short rain

does the old
bear stir
& potter
  about?
	the plum-flat
	  rock
	traversing
	outside sound
		grey &
		  dimmed
		scythed &
		  sheared of
		  light
			a protracted
			statement
			the long
			sentences

a dark
treaty with
  the major
ocean in the
  earth
	noiseless &
	magnetic
	  a long &
	narrow boat
		underground,
		manufacturing
		all possible
		  stories
			a new
			non-metal
			place

Mesostics: Two Boats

THE
rinsing moving shallow S ound-traffic, Lisson Grove to
bordered with small l A lperton, Grand Union
-nes of fast peopu L evel canal thru
double so to the wake of the diese L ondon, as tho' outside & in. Those slow can
The sun is dail Y ons of brick, of bread
grinding & arcing each way A nd bottle; a threaded stem of tunnel.
-round the tall tow N ot open to ghost-lands,
making the green water-plai N ot really a place of
light aft A dvice

THE
roaring wan D rawing Sun
pronounces the foot & the ivor I nhabits the gulfs & the coarse brown
God in forehead s O vens of the land with
the twist of his ski N oxious sound, where the
shines along the furr Y ellowed forms of the earth
shoulders, in the yard S hape & run in the grand
, courts, pylons, yo U nclosed sea-trees, in tawny
play for jug S andscape

The Wind-Cheer

Who
Volcanic

Who
Loosely
by the room-columns

the dials

in the sleek rain
and in the work-shots

shared air.

The pick-combed bridges
of joy-white paint-plaits
shined

this human
this truthful paint

two-line stops.
make it:
white/
check/
box/
water

how – ?
how many – (think forwards) –
dimensions!

a mill of people
a brisk air flowing
an Oxford road
a first sign of air
a turn of mouth

a quick-word
a word of technology

the eyes
don't care how

in a basement
all bits of mirrors
eyes
of fetishes,
neat, all neat

it's a
universal
intention

telly
to
the rich arcs
of private
visual poetry

the route –
the nose –
the repeat

bricks –
scenarios

brains –
passages

search.
sure.
badge.
balance.

the slot of tyres
& the regimen

shadow
and wig,
endless track
of tuned trees,
that the barrel

care, and be cute
for in the demon

the lover
at his boats
the heaven-hill / hell-mount
course
of the ballad

make pass
in the air

INcorporeal

cast

leap-sight

arm-arc — actuate

the blue of the back
the grey of
light

drive-in
sit-out
show-through

the hook-up
of air
of shaped air

ahead

Larry,
you was very close to

and the wreck
of the waltz,
the trip of the sight,
the step

a patrol
of this colour,
that colour

blank
bland
blow – hay

round in the road

tips –

takes the attention

sez look
sez
itz a whirlwind

a pocket
temp'-wind

two-foot-round

ten-foot-passed

he
drives-through

see!

on the cuttest hottest
day

and in Wessex

a little spire
of wind

a cone

of the chin
of the atmosphere

a joke

of the tablature.

Five-Liners

The brush and tap of the twigs,
Things wind-rolled, then at a standstill
(The sounds we usually strain out)
The coming-up of an animal, a predator,
And outside, the monstrous approach and departure.

This man is wanted for questioning
Staring in/at photo
Do not let
Be sure to ring
And Dead or Alive

'Humane conditions'
The great grey blanks of sides
As long, as for ever, as a pyramid.
Matching the shifting, sliding sand,
Guarding the living body.

Who are you looking at, SPROUTS?
Shut up, ROOTS!
Pay up, or get out of my garden!
Yes, I mean you, Mr Broccoli.
I'm keeping an eye on you, TREE.

Let me pay a tribute to Isocracy.
It assumes
A system of equality
In which all the members
Are human beings. (See also Demonocracy)

All the rolls of pebbles
Are rhythms,
Excruciatingly complex patterns,
Of millions of years
Of training. A refrain.

A particularly pretty girl

Holding an orange tin.
Not what she looks like,
Or what she says,
But the voice, how it shines and tangs.

In the great light-checked forest,
A party tracks our trees
And shoots them.
It is hard work for the hunters
Whose strange horns tangle in the dead wood.

What religion are you?
I offer him some farm cheddar cheese.
Perhaps my interrogator prefers unpasteurised goat?
In desperation,
I bring out the bright Stilton I got in Salisbury Market.

A goat
Riding on a dragon
And playing a pipe:
A dance?
A carol. maybe.

When the Jesuit
Interrogated the shepherds
He asked how many Gods they recognised?
One of them knew at least a 100,
Another speculated 'About a thousand?'

Hatless
We stand in the snow.
Someone great is rumoured to be passing.
Sure enough, on the dot of twelve,
A New Year has arrived.

The plates of the boat are in the mud.
The wheel is in my hand.
What next, captain?
He checks carefully on the chart,
And we roll cigarettes.

The rules of school confuse the child.
I explain,
It doesn't matter.
The bus is late.
I wait in the disfigured town centre.

Oggi-oggi-oggi!
Shouting at the shower,
Screaming at the sleet,
Fucking under thunder.
Oi Oi Oi!

The teams spill onto the field
A flood of colour.
Gorgeous, exulting flame-brown colour.
All the patterns of football –
And in colour!

So what will you pay me for being good?
Good at lying?
Or loving?
Or lurching into work?
No, just generally, being good.

Flying in the door.
Flying in the light.
NO REWARD.
Flying out the light.
Flying out the door.

Just a smooth yellow sea
Flat in the sun
Quite, quite empty.
Sunny,
And bravely light.

But the majesty of the WHOLE ...
A chorus of heart-crossing work,
A great ball of feeling.
A maze of giant song.

Shining windows, and dust, and lots of drink.

End.
Why so much ink?
He is creative, of course.
Oh.
Get him to clean it up, will you?

At Castleton

(for two simultaneous voices)

1	2
Some	
up on an alp	pause
sheep-balancers	and
by scant green	march
and top grey crops	and swaying hair
lime stone screestone	polished with wear
& rolling their cars down the pass	with knees and tabs
cycling them up	brown as ground
climbing, calling them over	like buns of Sun

                at CASTLETON   [1 & 2]
(A fossil fish at £1.95 but that ranks as a luxury)   [1 or 2]

Cards from Cologne

The *Prinz Philippe* at Dover Western Docks and 2 loads parcels (Royal Mail) are loaded thru the stern and there is a dazzling sun-deflexion of chalk shore-line, then cloudier over the camps and institutions of the shore.

*

Not so very full, for a ferry, and lots of secular freight can't be loaded, I note. There is quite a heavy coast-wind from the west, and delays for dockers' freight-ban on the miners' behalf, till after an hour, more, we move out turn the arms of the harbour walls.

*

Onto the broad, one-coloured sea, a slow, smoky diesel way, smooth across, I'm sitting in the shelter of the deck-works, or walking round the map of the ship, interested to see if it all joins up.

*

At Story Time, I've heard, when Noah's Ark was built, an extra pair of horses stowed away on board, and yes they were discovered but they wouldn't apologize to Noah and so they were thrown overboard and their sons & daughters are the white-haired waves everyday on the sea.

*

In the corridor of the train thru Belgium, all the no-smoking measures was a topic of conversation, & how it promoted Islam just like in Toronto the same sort of thing is a Christian crusade, as tho' the cities are everywhere avoiding people.

*

Passed thru the flatness of Belgium, the curved lovely lime-like hills above Verriers, then the water-land of the Rhine, and thru non-major chasms to Köln.

*

A new strange, standard, proper city, this wide-bridged Cologne, or a Roman re-settlement, it has a hedgehog cathedral.

*

Our room is on the ringroad, here called Sachnsenring which has at one end the Ulrepforte with its cone-hat, at one the Severinstorburg, a housed-over castle.

*

Look, this is the Pentáleon, an early Saalkirche, a hall church, broadened thru pierced walls & aisles, fountainous with its outside Westwerk.

*

A balcony, a royal chapel, overlooks the hall, all is whitely lit-up with film-lights, for a broadcast, showing one or two brave late extravagances, a multi-marble pulpit & altar-pile, under much gold.

*

A pause in the rain, outside the Pentáleon, the trees still shaking with wet, and the scented grass, like a new taste.

*

In the Andreaskirche, they are saying Angelus, some of it is chant, some is hymns, and each building holds a fragment of some Body.

*

The cathedral! this front, soft & light in the rain, this front sloped & leaning in the light, over, this front, pipes & tunnels, ringing in the wind, and as the pressure lightens, a front of flags & staffs.

*

Between the churches it has been no very long walk, but a lot of rain, discoveries are hidden in rebuilding, like glimpses of riding soldiers.

*

Now giant hail strikes Münich, and on Monday Dover will shut down, no more ferries from Monday morning, so it is necessary to re-book, on guess-work.

384

*

Once an oval mausoleum, a Roman tomb, but a decagon now, tall and arched, Roman Christian soldiers lay here, the Gereonkirche now in renovation.

*

At the top of the cap, by cap I mean the vault of the decagon, a boss, a golden sun, with golden tears or drops all coming out from it.

*

Meanwhile Zapf in his studio is also crying, the glue, the medium, of the colour, working on the eyes, and there are a bold, coursed & coloured triptych and titanic rollers for linocuts.

*

Round the room, a skeleton of sticky-taped sticks, dried free-twigs with knob-ends, spears or shafts, and other loose vraisemblences, with colour periodically banded on.

*

In the Rautenstrauch-Joest Museum, a shaped room-full in invocation, fetishes, rotted wood, lines of them, whole bags of nails rammed in, messages.

*

Eyes, contacts, tacks, mirrors.

*

There is a strange unbreathing spirit over the dark Rhine, as if anyone could move a city, der traurige Auspuff eines Autos, making directions in the dark.

*

Sunday, the Longericht Market, still raining, even in this variety of graveyard, of few stalls, shadow-puppets, cards, comix, beer-krugs, I go to Aachen.

*

For 'Ecce universa terra coram te', 'to enjoy the earth', Patronius tat … was er will.

*

Aachen, over-loved city, sprung with hot sulphurous water, Charlemagne's Pfalz woz here, his the chapel that still stands.

*

It is roughly round, it is multi-arcaded, it is top-lit, in a clearstage, wrought with all the columns he could come by.

*

Wilhelm Two remade it, he donated the marble to clothe it all, black mosaics to cover every patch of wall else, now respecting the debate on Wilhelm's sanity, it is decisive.

*

To see up on its imperial level is the problem, Charlemagne's throne on an upper floor, the tours are intermittent & arbitrary, where men are strangers on earth.

*

Why is it so guarded? what irks them so? It is just a plain stepped stone seat, not sighted to the hall-floor, a place on its own to take oaths & tie them.

*

At the altar-rail defile, they are skillfully extracting tips: 'Pony-soldaten?! WOAH … zwei Weisse! Lasst sie nicht fliehen!

*

Ah! who keeps the nations bound in place? What is all the commendatio, dominatio? What are the Christian Princes thinking of, to play about with perfection?

Ecclesiasticus ch. 14 etc.

Every kind of animal likes its own sort: every person appreciates his double.
Animals choose others of their own species to be with: people, too, stick
with their own kind.
How can a wolf be friends with a lamb? So it is between the unjust and
the just.
What agreement is there between the hyena and the dog? What sympathy
between the rich and the poor?
Lions feed on wild asses in the desert: the poor are the very grass the rich
feed on.
Failure and lack of ambition are hateful to the successful man: so a poor
person is hateful to the rich.
A rich man when things go wrong: is supported by his friends;
but a nobody in the same position: is rejected, especially by his friends.
When an important man falls: there is much sympathy;
he makes up impossible excuses: and people listen to him.
Someone of little account gets into trouble: and everyone turns on him;
he tells the truth about it: and is given no chance to repeat it.
When a wealthy man speaks: everyone maintains respectful silence;
anything he says: is praised to the sky.
A poor man speaks out: they say 'Who does he think he is?'
If he makes a slip: it won't be passed over ...

But those who see nothing but gold: cannot be called admirable
And those who demolish: will find they have their fill of it ...

Yetzer, the evil tendency: fills the valley like mist:
when the ungodly curse Satan, they curse their own souls,
for our imagination is round us: to make evil unaided ...

The man that builds his house: with other men's money
is like someone gathering stones: not wood for winter fuel ...

Virtually he kills his neighbour: who makes him unemployed ...

One is easy building: another pulling down;
what advantage is it to either? Nothing but endless work.

The Battle

Pride fleet choked in the fog
on the Altsee afloat
keen to listen
where some matching navy might be, in the mist.
In the figure of a ringed bull
it sits in the water –
now an explosion,
orange steel bathes it bit by bit.

the slice fluor'tange'-yellow
in about / against the undergrowth green
So my sudden son
made known & 'switten

The retching of the sea
a yellow-green warrior
jazz of its battering

fires on its surface
soul-flares

the gunners
smelling of lemons
were lost first
with the cordite-explosions

said it was Adventure
that was time-trap

Words

Words, by which (I mean)
agreements.

Avoidances:
horse-leaf-time
ear-being
thunderer

and Voids:
no – for –

without agreement,
how good, bad, ugly, empty!

Alf

A figure in a sealess ship

ROPES

hauling the sky

sometimes, stock-still, a tree

Promoted to a stone ...

With a head of candelabrum
to on-time mist-piece cue
CLUE

South Songs

Rejoice, join
be a Jute –
are people of water, corn-land,
oil-hills, work-towns;
made mazes, end-thickets,
walls in bald yellow-punched broom,
broad-roads.
ships, at a 1000 a week,
bring in stories
bonk sand-bells,
team with lorry-lights
and to be turf to football on,
roofs to bed under.

One of the 4 beasts saying
Come & see!
a white horse
and a crown
the noise of thunder
as it were
take peace
wheat at a penny
three measures
a great sword
under the altar
for the testimony
rest yet.

Robigalanus

'red dead garden'
lame flame flower
firey wiry damp
yellow billow peppermint
cold rolled barley
white fright wheat
hornet garneted godhead

Sound Stanzas

Someone is shovelling stones:
Wind and stones
are what I hear

Absent
except for their voices.
Young people, birds.

Strands from the cherry
inform even the
slowest heart.

This lute-nosed cream-ply blossom
'clining to yellow to pollen
big, scenic with scent

I cherish the fossil:
it is a gleam-ribbed trilobite.
I lay it on the computer.

shrimps
questions
clear from clear

Riddles

and step and stein and strain and shine and shift and still and shape and
straight and storm and show and strange and STONE

and soft and share and sail and shrine and shell and shriek and sand and
sea and shrimp and save and shore and SHIP

Speedway
(after Sprouts Elder)

These are word thoughts.
Over the cat-flanx of our guts,
broadsider is hide is sky-square
az the expert teeth grin
in the lid; safety checks.
Hid I the kind ears
& the wheat-dunlop-power-hair
oily-lined
to set up lips on gears, demon,
vivid iza space of sockets,
eye-spirals,
they do the work,
bursting in orange,
never seen tho', jacket'd in fins,
the word-work.

The harmony
izan ever-race
and that foot frict on the dirt-track,
on the horns the old-level arms
Lions, 2-tons, hold a balance
leg-tie
tilt
till it and all frame and spine
chime

A real flavour,
broken, cinders, scorch,
the acid in it a white line.
Testify –
the stern strenuous luck-fight
light into black,
blind out again,
round and flare back,
striking, rolling, lightning, spinning out.
dig him out –

see —
his smile is the real article
it's no carnival.
Had a noise race, ratio, kresh,
how it howled up,
uncanny / recognise
that it (red/blue/yellow/white and) start now.
The factors are speed (acceleration), reliability
and noise
lots of it, blasting, a deafening singing, A-Z,
a bowled-in of sound —
slow corners, straights, quick, bounding up
thumping and clapping,
into one last long note.
And the others are whining.

Then I cut back,
aligned,
opened it up,
broadsided,
tight in,
this foot down,
this leg hooked, holding,
coming out right,
and the straight again,
at full.

so hurt
bonked my head
back and back again on the wall
till I blacked out

It is the intermittence —
life switch beat
& heart-heat
THERE —

Leathers: blue pearls.
In the grid / grill
In the mesh / the cage

my mate, Tiger, sizes himself up,
a 'hairy' ride.
Yep, that slays us.

Lined up,
like two tags or teams,
getting a special colouring some way
then the band beats an anthem out,
you know, big oval notes for looking serious on.

key-commodity
simplicity.

My shale-life.
Scale:
greyhounds and speedway:
grey shades to cinders:
to black.
Wetted:
and look it grows (when skid)
upinto a black shower
and nightfirework (anti-lights)

WHAT IS IT? WOLF
or with a shake of sweat from the eyes OR LYNX OR
laugh to be left laying SOMETHING?
twisted under the frame, panting FORCE
derisions, defiance for the bruises THE PELT AWAY
try rise, heaving into black.

The competing,
making ultimate self
limitless
each BEST
all MOST

great break / burst of oil
searing the hot cylinder / the cylinder ribs
black cape on the shoulder tips
  age-dust to forearms

shadowing the jeans
welding and bike and owner
its heavy carbon
all but life-holding
grease-coat and oil-hymn

The sexual deception
of smell

But no brakes
is smooth

Postcard

At Cerne –
the downland paths
crowded with rude yellow weed
ceding to pale holiday bells
and birthday stars
all in the turf.
But the giant is out of it
cloud-bound
in the cheek of the hill.

The Flood
(found text for three voices)

1	2	3
promenade, the	us	and
rain	it was	on the
the January	nothing	
In	Arthur	the window
and we	hot tea	in a bread
Grimsby	my	He was
and	police houses	fishermen's
network of	mostly	families,
a deckhand	on the distant	brother
had been	in the	On the day
Dougie	up	clung
shrieking	dragged	
struggle		
The wind	all	crowded
fishermen	come	breaking
The	steamed	tobacco
counter	sports	box
and	and	and
Brewer.	and joked	his
being safer	cod	
of		
As darkness	veer	The noise
deafening	the wireless	waves
pier	thudding	reinforced
heat and	arguing	sea
bets	the iron	vibrating
	whilst	
to fly	inland	
decided		
him hammer	place	bars were
of	our feet	eddies

fixed
the
between
the narrow cut

coats
thumping

I
separated
our

The tide
a fire

washed
at
to pile

wind
back
to get
people

The quiet

the
armchairs
swarmed

the
street

Later
sky

the top
sands

hit
to a
arcades
from the sea

green
ground

the low
from
uncontrollably

wall at
and
furniture

by
yelled
at

candles
chimney

the first

emptying
ornaments
circles
food

help
black

yellow
At the
next market
scrambled
embankment

smashed
the
railway
and

into
the cliff

that
skin
the

had lit
the lights
the walls

Mrs
her husband
rose and fell

squalls
we saw
flickered
and
guttered

houses ... pumping

I

wading

seaweed
The
cloud were
bobbed

uprooted
right along

Moretum 2

Ow!
half-silent
the tumbrils of coffee and tea
(half-loud)
march round the cup/kettle
swirling early fog
as if some marsh of elder elves, say
Can I see my toes?
I canna?
Ah, ready.
Gold doiley lamps light up,
news starts,
bang bang bang!
for mud and metal
I part the legs of the cutlery,
sussurating, oh hump-back bacon,
dagger and drum, and tackle it,
this kitchen-time.

Elvis Sets Sail

Bella, the sea.
Out of the wide home harbour, tugs wrestle us
thru the host of friend-arms.
Elvis away!

Out on
On the history-sea
the mystery of supernatural fact!

And say the Sea is haunted –
what tunes, to sing to?
there, scratched gliss'es of water-wood
how does it all sound, under water?

The seeds of peace
stirred into the fertile furrow.

The mud-million
slowly and slowly mo' imperfe't
re-forming
re-growing (unshowing)
slowing

Wd not, wd not
walk up
empty stairs
stairs from the bed
and the sea-bed

How can you think it's tradition?
Greying the body, head into casque, all
to extirp the living race. Well,
AM I A DOG'S HEAD?   [2 Sam.
It's alright too, OK, we can whack a baseball,
run guest-machines on trial, sport in the sun and
the night, dark-rangers bidding the challenge,
alert, on alarm. Sugar-crumbled cities,

plains dead for beasts, root-cellars and towers,
stricken to tooth-hollow, admire the souvenirs,
bent-gone giants' what-they-left.
But no life.
A land an empty room.
Thoughtless. Us. And waving in colours!

To serve my country
I have to do it with drugs?
Soljer-chum, full of, try this then –
what do I want to taste that for?
WHAT MORE CAN I DO TO MY VINEYARD?   [Isaiah
threshing about us
– no candy on the tree
shouting about
– no gold on the corn-stalk
Plague is on us again!
– tar-jawed!
– boil-eared!
The awful
– umbrella
– of rain
enribs us all
and
The wet bodies
– are wasted
we fade

Be-listen me!
I ran the desert.
It was thick with the fingers of law-dead dreams,
forked phantasies, blood-green growing.
Displaced and marbled bends of magpie
ricked the cliffs, and sabbath sun
tricked its nugget-brothers up into a shine.
Coca and blow-candy, banana-vision
misled me like grave-lights, and I heard (all)
the chorus of tang-bells, eye-bells, air.
Who is the high-shrine at the border?
Will we lose it at the last?

Grow to the water, get rich,
franchise a free whim,
invent the kitten, praise children, endorse
and define the processing of the ill
or end up all alone?
GO INTO THICKETS,
will you, CLIMB UP UPON THE ROCKS?   [Jeremiah

These are the CHERUBIM,
TWO, TOUCHED ONE ANOTHER
THE WING OF ONE & THE WING OF THE OTHER,   [1 Kings
taller than the doors,   (Solomon's
& spread gildy-glint boundary to boundary   Temple)
and bright-shirted
and headed by the special God-craft.
Lovelier than lettuce or rodeos,
broader than ship-spans,
at arm-grip at their temple-task.
I ask
what language they spoke?

Let the humble carrot
lead us.
Boxes of spinach
preach.
Out of the mouths of navy-blue aubergines
and plums,
take note
of the law,
it flickers like a tomato-tongue,
its rule is radish.
THE CHILDREN
SHALL BE OLIVE-PLANTS   [Ps.128
Good is the palm-hat,
the gloves of rhubarb,
the cucumber-train.
At the melon-disco,
we will dance and judge.

LET ALL WHO ARE FAT

EAT & ADORE. [Ps.22
Diggers are gold.
They weave and sift the soil,
hem a ditch,
All-belabour, straining
bronze britches,
laugh with sloped women,
sink, grub up, pink, graft, prod
and grow fat.

Live thru / think back.
The time of it confirms itself, buddy-bowl,
full-tape, growing and plays and too takes in,
it's all sense / acceptance.
Hand-to-hand we chain and keep place, on
the sticky goose, no bizarre spoons to swallow,
no melting throat,
a tent of beaded rays, please,
somewhere to haunch-down, try a run
of chords on the ear, look cute.
LET ME HEAR JOY & GLADNESS,
MAKE THE BONES YOU BROKE BE HAPPY. [Ps.51

My body? Did you know I was a half-breed?
Rubbery and cleaned, loose cotton-puppet-sticks,
rarely our skin, Apache-smooth,
slightly, boldly, tanned.
It is a sign in which kids walk in the sun,
and learn we are warm matter, and
see in the black mirror of me the
chance to jig, make air,
read
muscle.
Like a can-opener.
Scout-cows lick for the salt,
ke-hote-es tumble and scent the dark,
WILL DEATH FEED ON ME? [Ps.49

Aristeas' Journal

In the seventh century BC a Greek traveller called Aristeas seems to have made a journey into Scythian territory, roughly where Romania is situated today. He finally reached the edge of the Carpathian mountains, where he hoped to find a race called the Hyperboreans, whom, it was rumoured, were specially blessed by Apollo and lived in a golden age of peace and contentment.

Evan Hadingham

Like as in Greek democracy
I wasn't voted or elected
but picked by a chance,
lotted to seek out knowledge: starts and meanings

I found many fragments

Sea-veined
sky-gloved
star-haired
every heir
and all
settling
to be the world.

He says he lays him, acts horizon, has the quick earth power to back,
She says an arch, she will arch her' like a packet-sky, to be earth-over.
And he rises
She opens
A rehearsal of how to make
Make / to Do.
Warm world living about
Between the two, still.

Two codes
two keys
Certainty
Stability
The all million-long continuity

(like races of ferns)
Handling complexity
Admitting variety / unpredictability
(all the potential & quasi-new pattern of an unrolling carpet ...)

One moment there is wheat, then a wave.
In a rush you trust some people
But they are a cold window to.
You had better save your
loyalty sez the sandstone figure.
But what then?

Then we are as of but a
cold wall
          ahead us,
where we 'ttack & break at
with dumb knobs
like we could burst beyond,
see the halls and homes others share in.

Or
bead and rod
everything to a trust
a joy
and a world-crush.

OR
what holds us?
(faintly painted
pictured together in a time)
Nothing?
(walking to the next adventure, room to room)
(Just lots of tunes to listen to)
(A dangerous floor)
(It is a good game)
(It is a bitter drink Eve served.)
(It is not like being a football fan.)
(It is like being tuned in to the rain.)

These are the wrestlers of agony

dislocating their ankles,
tearing, in a pair, in terror, yelling,
squeezing, sick in the struggle
to annihilate,
pull open the puzzle, WHAT IS IT? WOLF
or with a shake of sweat from the eyes OR LYNX OR
laugh to be left laying SOMETHING? FORCE THE PELT AWAY,
twisted under the victor, panting derisions, FORCES
try rise, heaving into black. BLOOD FROM THE VEINS

Body-verbs
that are muscle, that are moving,
to lever shaft to shaft; to guard, to grow,
Blood-fed the bulge of the arm pulls up
/ anchors
or the leg folds & straights to run.

To move,
maybe that is most.

The warm-beef breast
The war-polyp
and the springing breast
the mare's-tail-eye
all woven and worked;
faces, fellows, for settling toward,
lass, sows love,
hearts, bread, together speaks
yeast-herd

A leg-ring
a wrist-bone
a chain
as tho' you can box-up action
unwire the arteries
& still be classed sensate

Lacking sexuality to violence;
more when its risk arose
between units that could or would not breed

a speci-al or political obliteration.

Why the world! – a regime of calamity
      (At your imagined –
Where each subject thing risks its neck
      (coming to impossibility

(Today
    Lit by the little bunkers of gas,
    I wait,
(The competing is
    the whole room square senses,
    what is settling, coiled,
    the great, quartz-scaled snake-being
    of the cold
    tight & bright
    so when I bed, mid-black,
    that will be soccy,
    boox, flowers and I,
    in the race to reptile,
    the stately unheated hole.
(Today
The competing
's over.

And by the fields
red & raisiny, a blur
that are people to run

Against the sky-etch / snow-arch
snow-land at football,

the	RUNS	footballer
all turn	SKIDS	like a herd
roused	SHOOTS	in tremble
alert	YELLS	ice-active

ice-show-er
surges forward / scents it, the
22-footed dragon coils itself to goal
will (to) trick the goal-girl
in her adverts (it is of a, the, same)

loudness of body-drama
& the spring of the action
the snowy steaming crowd.

The Hittites invented letters
but it was the skalds linked words
like gold-rose-wrists of new-shirt-smartness,
Or goddess-tears (for rain) and share-singer

The lovers
like wrapping a parcel

   caring and folding
   these are the leaves of lettuce

   a smattering of diamond light
   still in a box, perhaps

   but a glowing pepper-burn
   rubs teeth & boot, breath, belly

   accepts, receives,
   folds, saves, rolls rose-in-like (lives)

A crisp route,
mountains,
parallels of rock, shine-faced,
austere & sun.
A pass. I pass. Loose-slide.
I will make it.
Interviews with Hyperboreans
in their cloud-rooms, coming.

The dust's shipped
on the earth-shoulder;
the barbarian
is grass now
& the knees 'come bricks.
The mists ring us,
are vertebrae, star-bones,

a sensational rising.

That we dissolved, awake,
was show-token
would you think you one –
more a collar of tawny orbs,
star-board
that incessant bless,
patrol to one, will-less &
king-loud

flesh-loquent
the air-buds arrange
new compounds, old word & new word
a juggling cups, beans
tumbling, shipping to the dust
mazed as mute as complete

From *A Pocket History of the Soul*

In the supplement
a collection, cut-outs,
on thin paper, some 200,000 soljers,
trembling where they stand,
usher them to place 'it's like herding sheep'; [1]
stiffer card for the republican guard,
'they are very good soljers, very good soljers,'
and one small plastic Saddam,
moustached,
venomous.
As an experiment,
80,000 of the thin ones
are turned to ash.
We want to leave 'a tidy desert'. [2]
They do not dance, yell, pray,
they have no souls of course,
these inanimate soljers.
'They're not part of the same human race.' [3]
   More substantial
I dredge our own boys
out of the bottom the cornflake packet.
And array them.
Some grasp miniature roll-ups of the Sun.
They have been unemployed; and orphans;
but led by multi-named shoots of very respectable wombs.
But are they –
Disturbed,
I rattle them, this-one/that-one, this-one/that-one
– oh, no souls!
Careless! irresponsible manufacture, dangerous,
ridiculous!
   The leader cowers under a table.
Fortunately perhaps, it is a strong table.
Conceptually,
it could be a table-cloth,
bearing up molten sand.
Each self would then be the same,
soul-shorn.

How can I tell which is worth more?
How can I recognise, for example,
now I've got all the cardboard out –
the Sheriff of the World?
　　Is it for democracy
or against democracy?
(They have not put an Emir in the packet at all.)
Or is there
no option –
pray you please the God,
fight-bezeek him,
that He pass
to you the right soul at last.
　　Fortunately, in this chest,
I keep the Holy Reproduction.
Stand by,
you love-jug
be-beaded with bridges/hearts,
word-spans, rivers of revels,
capstans, knot-bands, colour –
empty, bright, ready!
　　Who will bring joy to Ireland?
Hawaii? th'Ukraine? Tibet?
And who will feel the cord of history
round their neck?
Then stay in the toy-box,
if you wunna
pay tuppence for honesty –
paya penny for a soul.
　　The skull-man
has broke
out the flowerpot,
the biscuit
is happy in my gut,
the crown of crowns
blazes
in the Tower.

1 Brit. Officer 27.2.91
2 BBC News 10.3.91
3 Gen. Schwarzkopf 27.2.91

Les Assis (after Rimbaud)

Men
to be mole-dark,
placard-skulled,
rough-bright beaches of fungi.

We echo
and
stand.

Some Ossianic fantasy?
of limb-sticks,
bold tokens
of twist to rung.

Special,
dim,
brittle.

What else – to sit,
perking skin,
before the vitreous symbols,
intending.

Winter
with-
stand.

And the chairs grow:
being wood and sun,
wheat and light,
all inter-twinned.

Sooner
Sun
simple.

Crouch, play,
drum,
like clapping-songs,
and all null love.

Signal
and
issue.

Don't do it!
They are cats awake,
wilful and hombrous,
full-inflate!

Rise
to be
watched.

Bald,
black,
with faun-buttons
light-house-sharp.

Deliberate
with
colour.

Ever
dangerous,
all-broke fighters,
a-fume, a-trap, a-throat.

Who
is
seeing?

Notes

General abbreviations and bibliography:

Bikers, with John Muckle. London: Amra Imprint, 1990.

CEP: Collected Earlier Poems (1966-80), ed. Alan Halsey & Ken Edwards. Hastings: Reality Street, 2010.

Disc: BG collected poems compiled & issued electronically, 1991, rev. 1996.

ER5: Etruscan Reader 5, with Tom Raworth & Tom Leonard. Newcastle under Lyme: Etruscan Books, 1996.

FE: Future Exiles: 3 London Poets, with Allen Fisher & Brian Catling. London: Paladin, 1992.

MF: The Mud Fort. Cambridge: Salt Publishing, 2004.

PHS: A Pocket History of the Soul. Seaham: Amra Imprint, 1991.

TAG: A Tract Against The Giants. Toronto: Coach House Press, 1984.

TBD: A Text Book of Drama. London: Writers Forum, 1987.

TF: A Tour of the Fairground. Exbourne: Etruscan Books, 2007.

TT: Tyne Txts, with Tom Pickard. Seaham: Amra Imprint, 2004.

WNM: Worlds of New Measure: An anthology of five contemporary British Poets, ed. Clive Bush. London: Talus Editions, 1997.

All texts appear in *Disc* unless noted as e.g. 'MB only'.

Year of publication for undated items supplied by the bibliography compiled by Doug Jones and published in *The Salt Companion to Bill Griffiths,* ed. Will Rowe (Cambridge: Salt Publishing, 2007).

Further Songs & Dances of Death

First edition, an A5 pamphlet, 12pp, published by Anarcho Press, London 1982.

Materia Boethiana [MB]

First edition published by Galloping Dog Press and The Poetry Bookshop, Newcastle and Hay-on-Wye 1984. Quarto, duplicated mimeo, 30pp printed rectos only.

19. 'Scenario' / 'Alfred's Metre'. *MB* only.

22. 'Karl Schmidt's Boethius Version.' *MB* only. The reference is to Karl Heinz Schmidt *König Alfreds Boethius-Bearbeitung,* Göttingen: Süddruch, Göttingen-Reinhausen, 1934.

25. 'Link One.' *MB* only.

25. 'Charm or Chant.' 'Chant' in *FE*. *Disc* notes 'this charm against police interrogation techniques uses tags from several Old English charms.'

30. 'Link Two.' *MB* only. The lines appear in *Disc* as the opening section of 'Guide to the Giants of England'.

31. 'Guide to the Giants of England.' *MB* text incorporating a few variants in *TAG*. The section beginning 'not fast' appears in *FE* as 'Birds (found text)'. *Disc* notes: '*smolt* (OE) i.e. mild'; *one clear morn* ... 'a lyrical quote from Mrs Thatcher'; *currently fashionable* 'the ref. is to Bord's book on giants'; 'the Chorea Gigantum, or dance of giants, was an early name for Stonehenge'; *heart the keener* ... 'quote from OE poem on Maldon'.

41. 'Alfred's Prose.' *MB* only.

42. 'November.' Reprinted in *FE* & *WNM*. *Disc* notes: *Migne's printing*: 'in *Patrologia Latina*'; Ice Maiden: 'Mrs Thatcher'; *viks* 'i.e. creeks, possibly origin of the name Viking'.

44. 'The Hawksmoor Mausoleum.' Text retains the section numbers of *MB* & *FE* but adopts the few minor revisions of *WNM*. *Disc* notes: *the cuckoo king* 'George VI, for obvious reasons'; section 13: 'Pharoah's Dream?'

49. 'Eight Barques for the Manifold Soul of G.L.Renfree.' Reprinted in *WNM* with addition of first stanza to section 4. Text retains *MB* layout. *Disc* notes: G.L.Renfree was BG's friend 'who died suddenly of narcolepsy'; the early poem 'Armageddon' was also written in his memory (see *CEP* p.16 and note) as was 'The Bournemouth'; section 4 'may be performed to the tune of the Streltsy chorus from Mussorgsky's *Khovanshchina*.'

54. 'Link Three.' *MB* only.

55. 'The Peacock Variations.' Reprinted in *MF*. *Disc* notes: 'a short-note version on Kodaly's work on the song in which a peacock flies over a prison.'

The Bournemouth

First edition published by Writers Forum and Pirate Press, London and Cowley 1987. 16pp.

Text follows *Disc*, a considerably revised and somewhat expanded version.

Disc notes: 'this sequence is somewhat modelled on Fitzgerald's stanza in the *Rubaiyat*. Following the loss of my father in 1984 I found myself thinking back to the earlier death of Gordon Renfree, for whom this was composed. The images are based on the south coast where Gordon grew up, but involve also death-journey symbolism and game-rituals of Etruscan source.'

The Book of the Boat

BB1: First edition published by Writers Forum, London [1988]. 26pp quarto. Text reproduced from BG's holograph and with drawings by BG.

BB2: Second edition published by Amra Imprint, Seaham [1991], reformatted in

A5 landscape, 52pp. The text in this reprint is reproduced from the same master copy but the sequence of both poems and visuals shows considerable variation; three texts are omitted and one visual added (see below). Our text follows the sequence of the first edition.

Although some of these poems appear in later collections in the customary lineation of most modern poetry we have followed BG's use in *BB1/2* of the older orthographic convention in which line-ends are marked by a full stop and additional letter-space.

76. 'Ballad of Blissworth Tunnel Open.' *Disc* notes 'this tunnel is on the Grand Union Canal.'

77. 'Spiller's Boat.' Reprinted with variant layouts and source noted as 'after Mary Norton's *Borrowers*' in *TBD* & *WNM*.

79. 'The Rabbit Hunt.' Reprinted in a slightly revised version with conventional verse lines in *ER5*. *Disc* dates 1986. The passage beginning 'the third day. leads us.' appears in conventional verse lines as 'The Trip Up The Stort' in *MF*.

84. 'My Boat is Burned ...' Omitted in *BB2*.

84. 'Archbishop Wulfstan ...' Omitted in *BB2*.

85. 'Brightlingsea.' Reprinted as 'The Festival' in *FE* & *MF* with the italicised lines shown as 3-line stanzas. *Disc* notes 'The technique is intended to be haiku in prose.' *FE* & *MF* include two additional stanzas preceding 'It's what roads are for': 'How can I be reassuring: there's no way round it all but movement. // Listen, Alf Pauline: / it isn't you that has changed / but the scene placed in.'

86. 'The Cimmerian.' Reprinted as 'Conan' with conventional verse lines in *MF*. *Disc* notes 'loosely based on the adventure "Red Nails".'

87. 'The Land-Search.' The paragraph 'Stretches of earth ...' is omitted in *BB2*, perhaps accidentally since it is restored in *WNM*. The *WNM* text appears as a single paragraph. *Disc* notes 'this is a sort of sci-fi text, but based on an actual trip to look at possible residential moorings that turned out to be far out in the wilds of Essex.'

90. 'Coast Notes.' Omitted in *BB2*, presumably because BG had by then reordered much of the poem in 'Morning Lands 1: In Essex' (see below).

91. Canal map added in *BB2*, inserted between 'The Cimmerian' and 'The Land-Search'. Replaced here for its relevance to the following 'Log'.

92. 'Log of the Cimmerian (prose).' *BB1* & *BB2* only.

93. 'Log of the Cimmerian (Sea-Shanties).' Reprinted with conventional 3-line stanzas in *FE* ('Sea Shanties') & *MF* ('Shanties', stanzas unnumbered).

99. 'The Marriage at Ipswich Docks.' Reprinted with conventional 3-line stanzas in *WNM* ('Nocturnes and Diurnes').

101. 'Unities.' Reprinted in a slightly revised version, with conventional verse lines and the stanza beginning 'Evidence a hump' omitted, in *FE* & *A Book of Legends*.

102. 'Closing Song.' Reprinted with conventional 4-line stanzas in *TT* ('At the

Stephenson Monument'), where the 6th line reads 'My folk are dead, the diesel lives' and the 8th 'In the dark start off for work.'

Morning Lands

ML1: First edition, with title hyphenated as *Morning-Lands*, published by Pirate Press, Cowley [1989]. Trimmed A5 landscape, 98pp printed rectos only, text reproduced from BG's hand-drawn outline script with lines written continuously as in Old English MSS, 'blocking in the last syllable of each "line" [i.e. of verse] as a halt.' (BG's note.) Includes dedication page: 'These poems are freely & friend-fully dedicated to Mark Wm. Harman of Little Clacton who hospitably provided me space to live & work in in 1988-9 after the boatyard that burned my house-boat felt disinclined to replace it.'

ML2: Second edition published by Amra Imprint, London [1991]. A5, 32pp, text reproduced from typescript with conventional verse lines. Dedication omitted.

The two editions show considerable variants, particularly in the ordering of the text. We have followed *ML2*, supported by *Disc*, since this is clearly BG's final version; occasional misprints have been corrected with reference to *ML1*.

105. '1: In Essex.' The most considerable variants are the inclusion in *ML1* of the first stanza of 'On The Nile' (see *A Book of Legends* below) following the line 'need never even know the noise'; and the omission of the passage beginning 'One yellow car' which reworks the second section of the 1970s poem 'Encomium Urbis – Colchester' (*CEP* p.160). The stanza beginning 'One way' appears in *MF* as a separate poem, 'Colchester'. Sections 1 & 4 had previously appeared in 'Coast Notes' (*BB1*, see above), as had stanzas 1, 3 & 4 of section 10.

113. '2: De Apio (Concerning Celery).' *ML2* revising *ML1* with some additions and extensive rearrangement of passage beginning 'A wind of death'. Stanzas 1-3 reprinted as a separate poem, 'De Apio', in *MF*. *Disc* notes that the poem 'is based at a Nursery at Little Clacton' and identifies the stanza beginning 'She found a cornflower' as a 'found text, from a children's book by Bernard Ashley.'

123. '3: With Pomona.' *ML2* makes a few additions and minor changes to *ML1*.

127. '4: Interiors.' *ML2* shows a few variants and additions to, as well as omissions from, *ML1*.

Poems after Plotinus

First collected in *On Plotinus [OP]*, an A5 pamphlet, 29pp, published by Amra Imprint, London [1990], where the poems were embedded in extracts from the *Enneads* in prose translations and were followed by a 'Commentary' consisting of extracts taken principally from Lyall Watson *Supernature* and Tompkins & Bird *The Secret Life of Plants*. For reasons of space our text follows *TF* in omitting the prose extracts. The order of the poems also follows *TF* (and *Disc*) although the Greek titles of *OP* are restored.

139. 'Peri tou Ekousiou kai Thelematos tou Enos.' Reprinted in *TF*.

142. 'Peri Pyseos kai Theorias kai tou Enos.' Line 24 follows revision in *TF*. Line 35 follows *OP*, reading 'prose' for 'prize' in *MF* & *TF* as misprint.

144. 'Peri Pronoias Proton.' Reprinted in *MF* & *TF*.

148. 'Peri Eudaimonias.' Reprinted in *WNM* & *TF*. Sections V & VI lineation as *OP* & *WNM*.

Darwin's Dialogues [DD]

First edition, an A5 pamphlet, 44pp, published by Amra Imprint, London [1991]. There were two issues with identical text but variant covers: the first is laminated, showing a drawing of the Natural History Museum, the epigraph from Weinberg and the dedication; the second is matt and shows a drawing of Plesiosaurus Dolichodeirus, omitting epigraph and dedication.

153. 'Opening.' *DD* only.

155. 'Josiah Wedgwood II & Robert Darwin.' *DD* only.

156. 'View.' In *Disc* the final line reads 'Ne confundebor!'

159. 'Josiah Wedgwood & Charles Darwin.' *DD* only.

161. 'Adventure (Found & New Text).' *DD* only.

165. 'Charles Darwin & The Sea-Captain.' *DD* only.

167. 'The Breed.' Reprinted in *WNM* with revision to stanza 14.

169. 'Darwin & The Finch.' *DD* only.

171. 'Steve's Garden.' Reprinted in *WNM* in the adjusted layout followed here. *Disc* notes 'for Steve Clews' garden at Hendon. The choruses are multi-voice and involve both unison and divided work.' The *DD* text includes meandering lines of dots to indicate circulation of voices.

182. 'Darwin & Wife.' *DD* only.

184. 'The Relief of Aachen.' *DD* only.

188. 'Darwin to Marx.' *DD* only.

190. 'Alternative Ending.' *DD* only.

A Book of Legends [BL]

First collected edition an A5 pamphlet, 31pp, published by Writers Forum & Amra Imprint, London [1991]. Our text omits 'Unities', previously collected in *BB1/2*.

Part One was first published as *Quire Book* by Writers Forum, London 1985 *[QB]*, with the poems untitled.

197. 'The Brothers.' Reprinted in *FE* ('The Bowmen') & *MF*.

200. 'Dance.' Reprinted in *MF*.

209. 'On the Nile.' *Disc* notes 'this is a version of a well-known story about the removal of the hidden store of bodies from the Valley of the Kings area.' The first stanza was added in *BL*. In *QB* the poem incorporates a passage beginning 'No / Christ straight / kid-clear' which was later included in the *Bikers* version of 'To Johnny Prez' – see *CEP* pp.358-9.

212. 'The Argosy.' Text follows *FE*. *BL* omits stanzas 7, 11 & 12 and the second half of 10.

215. 'Pattern-Peeps.' Reprinted in *FE*.

216. 'Brunnhilde & Me.' *BL* text. In *FE* the poem ends at 'then crooked in a fairy-wail.'

219. 'Metamorphoses.' Reprinted in *MF*. In line 10 'than' corrected to 'then'.

220. 'The Ship.' Reprinted in *MF*.

Coal

First published as three Writers Forum pamphlets, *Coal 1* in 1990, *Coal 2* & *Coal 3* in 1991.

Metrical Cookery

First published as an A5 pamphlet, 24pp, by Amra Imprint, London [1991]. *Disc* includes only a selection of these poems.

259. 'Moretum.' Reprinted in *WNM* ('Moretum 1'). *Disc* notes 'Moretum is a genre of Latin poem concerned with getting up in the morning and having break-fast (honestly)' and 'the quote is from an Old English text (Aelfric?).'

263. 'Cake.' Reprinted (first stanza only) in *MF*.

266. 'Citrus Note.' Reprinted in *MF*.

268. 'Egg Poem (Optional).' *Disc* notes 'dates from the great egg-scare and a Tory ministress's problems over the public perception of eggs.'

274. 'Pickle, The Pot of.' *Disc* notes 'an alternative recipe is provided by Keats.'

278. 'Tokaj.' Reprinted in *FE* & *MF*.

The Purple Shepherd

First edition published by Anarcho Press, London 1991, 13pp. Section numbers and some minor corrections supplied by *Disc*.

Disc notes:

285. '1. Aeschylus.' Second stanza quoted from *Cycle* 4 (*CEP* p.74).

289. '4. Boethius.' First stanza from Metre 27 of King Alfred's OE version of *The Consolation of Philosophy*.

292. '6. Nuttall.' Reprinted in *WNM* as 'For Jeff Nuttall'. Opening quote from Nuttall's *Bomb Culture*.

North Scenes [NS]

A miscellany of poems written between the late 1970s and 1991, collected as an A5 pamphlet, 20pp, by Amra Imprint, Seaham [1992]. 'Notes (Staithes/Whitby)' appears in *CEP* pp.287-8 and is omitted here.

297. 'Little Scenes.' *Disc*'s revisions and rearrangement of the *NS* text are followed here. 'First theorem' is an expansion of the 4-line poem 'Space' in *NS*. The sequence includes several much earlier poems: 'Bland bay roads around' ('North Shields', *CEP* p.31); 'So / the whole county ...' slightly revising 'Winter', *CEP* p.20; 'It seemed absurd ...' with revisions to 'At Stanley', *CEP* p.23. The *NS* version included 'Huck', *CEP* p.45, which also appears in whole or in part in several other poems and sequences.

305. 'In The Coal Year.' Reprinted in *FE* & *MF* (title misprinted as 'In The Coral Year'). *Disc* notes: 'this was written for the 1984-5 coal strike; it includes loosely found material from the liberation of Haiti'; 'SHE: Mrs Thatcher or any other dangerous force of nature.'

308. 'Moorsrider.' Text follows *FE*; there are slight variants in *NS* & *Disc*. *Disc* notes 'this series celebrates the one-day travel-around ticket in Cleveland; here by bus to Kirkdale, then north again via Whitby' and 'Wade's stone stands in a field north of Whitby'.

311. 'Sixteen Riddles.' Text incorporates some revisions (particularly the more specific answers) from *Disc*.

Joanne's Book [JB]

A miscellany of poems, mostly written in the 1980s, collected as an A5 pamphlet, 28pp, by Amra Imprint, Seaham [1993].

317. 'Dedication.' *Disc* title 'Bequest'.

318-319. 'The Tempest', 'The Toys', 'Ely', 'St Albans'. These four poems were written *circa* 1970. BG fragmented them with other early poems into 'War W/ Windsor Text 1 (4 Voices)' (*CEP* pp.113-4). *JB* was their first appearance in their original form.

320. 'In Yorkshire: Mark's Slide.' First published as 'Mark's Slide' in *FE*. *JB* title 'In Yorkshire'.

321. 'Joanne-Marie's Swimming Manual.' First published as an Apt Post broadside 1981. Reprinted in *TAG*. Text follows earlier versions, retaining the section titles, but adds stanza 'For the little one' from *JB*. *Disc* notes: 'Latin quote from early account of Loch Ness Monster'; 'Anglo-Saxon quote from *Beowulf*'; prose passage 'partly found text, originally composed separately for a project initiated by Paul Green', viz. *Variations: Various Artists* (Peterborough: Spectacular Diseases, 1985).

330. 'At the Junction with the Slough Arm.' Reprinted in *MF*.

330. 'Mark's Poster of Wales.' *Disc* title 'Wales'.

331. 'In The Car.' *Disc* title 'Road Works'.

333. 'One Hundred Images of a Captured Friend.' *Disc* dates to the early 1980s and notes that stanza 95 is 'from an Old English charm'. The *JB* text is misnumbered with two 28s, corrected by dividing 90 into 89 and 90: 'about talkless terror – / and who makes it // the diner / and the slaughterer'.

342. 'Now …' Revision of early poem 'Image', *CEP* p.32.

Other Poems

345. 'Prince Igor.' Not in *Disc*. Published anonymously as an A3 broadside without publisher or date but presumably one of the several broadsides BG issued in 1980-81; text reproduced from BG's holograph and with his hand-coloured illustrations. The poem is a treatment of Borodin's opera.

350. 'Songs (after Schubert).' *Disc* note: 'possibly a short-note version of *Winterreise*'.

353. 'Short Bestiary.' Collected in *TAG*. *Disc* adds final line to stanza 6 with note 'the original version of this evolved from some intriguing line of Lee Harwood's.'

355. 'Second Family Spell, Without Names.' Cf. 'Family Spell', p.326.

361. 'Grief that the Palestinians are Treated like a Tribe of Onions.' *PHS*, reprinted in *MF*.

362. 'Two Summer Poems.' Not in *Disc*. Published in *The Poet's Voice* 3 (Bath, 1983).

363. 'The GLC Abolished.' Collected in *FE*.

365. 'The Uxbridge Workers.' Collected in *FE*.

368. 'Untitled Poem for 4 Voices.' Not in *Disc*. Another anonymous broadside, A4, without publisher or date, text reproduced from BG's holograph & arranged diagrammatically.

370. 'At Matlock.' Not in *Disc*. Published with text reproduced from BG's holograph and arranged diagrammatically in *Figs* 13 (Matlock, 1987).

371-372. 'Exposition' & 'The Long Barrow'. Not in *Disc*. Published with text arranged diagrammatically in *Kite* 3 (Cardiff, 1989).

373. 'Mesostics: Two Boats.' Not in *Disc*. The poems appear on a pair of untitled A4 broadsides, without publisher or date. The texts were reproduced from BG's holograph and outline script, accompanied by hand-coloured drawings. Cf. 'The Waterfell', p.75.

374. 'The Wind-Cheer.' Published in *Figs* 13, 1987. Text follows the slightly revised version in *Disc*.

379. 'Five-Liners.' Text follows *FE* but inserts 4th stanza from *Disc*. *Disc* text ends with stanza beginning 'What religion are you?'

382. 'At Castleton.' Collected in *TBD*.

383. 'Cards from Cologne.' Not in *Disc*. Published in *Talus* 3 (London, 1988).

387. 'Ecclesiasticus ch. 14 etc.' Not in *Disc*. Published in *Mar* 1 (St Ives, 1989). All

contributions to *Mar* were anonymous. BG's prefatory note: '(I haven't had much experience at writing anonymous poems, but thought the enclosed, a version of a bit of Ecclesiasticus, might suit. It is a nice antidote to the usual Christian sense of euphoria, achievement etc., which is probably why it was rejected from the Bible itself.)'

390. 'South Songs.' Published in *Other: British and Irish Poetry since 1970*, ed. Richard Caddel & Peter Quartermain (Hanover & London: Wesleyan UP, 1999).

390. 'Robigalanus.' *Disc* note: 'The opening line is a quote from Thomas A. Clark.'

392. 'Speedway.' Collected in *Bikers* & *MF*. *Disc* note: 'This is based on the book *The Romance of Speedway* by Sprouts Elder (1930)'.

395. 'Postcard.' Published in *fragmente* 3 (Oxford, 1991).

398. 'Moretum 2.' Collected in *WNM*. Cf. 'Moretum', p.259.

399. 'Elvis Sets Sail.' Collected in *ER5*, *Disc* adding Biblical references.

403. 'Aristeas' Journal.' Collected in *FE*, *Disc* adding the stanzas beginning 'To move' and 'The warm-beef breast'.

409. 'From *A Pocket History of the Soul.*' *PHS* only.

411. 'Les Assis (after Rimbaud).' First published in *Soleil + Chair: a commemoration of the centenary of Arthur Rimbaud*, ed. Harry Gilonis (London: Writers Forum 1991). Reprinted in *ER5*. Text follows the revised or corrected version in *ER5*.

Alphabetical List of Titles

REALITY STREET titles in print

Poetry series

Kelvin Corcoran: *Lyric Lyric* (1993)
Maggie O'Sullivan: *In the House of the Shaman* (1993)
Allen Fisher: *Dispossession and Cure* (1994)
Fanny Howe: *O'Clock* (1995)
Maggie O'Sullivan (ed.): *Out of Everywhere* (1996)
Cris Cheek/Sianed Jones: *Songs From Navigation* (1997)
Lisa Robertson: *Debbie: An Epic* (1997)
Maurice Scully: *Steps* (1997)
Denise Riley: *Selected Poems* (2000)
Lisa Robertson: *The Weather* (2001)
Lawrence Upton *Wire Sculptures* (2003)
Ken Edwards: *eight + six* (2003)
Redell Olsen: *Secure Portable Space* (2004)
Peter Riley: *Excavations* (2004)
Allen Fisher: *Place* (2005)
Tony Baker: *In Transit* (2005)
Jeff Hilson: *stretchers* (2006)
Maurice Scully: *Sonata* (2006)
Maggie O'Sullivan: *Body of Work* (2006)
Sarah Riggs: *chain of minuscule decisions in the form of a feeling* (2007)
Carol Watts: *Wrack* (2007)
Jeff Hilson (ed.): *The Reality Street Book of Sonnets* (2008)
Peter Jaeger: *Rapid Eye Movement* (2009)
Wendy Mulford: *The Land Between* (2009)
Allan K Horwitz/Ken Edwards (ed.): *Botsotso* (2009)
Bill Griffiths: *Collected Earlier Poems* (2010)
Fanny Howe: *Emergence* (2010)
Jim Goar: *Seoul Bus Poems* (2010)
James Davies: *Plants* (2011)
Carol Watts: *Occasionals* (2011)
Paul Brown: *A Cabin in the Mountains* (2012)
Maggie O'Sullivan: *Waterfalls* (2012)
Peter Hughes: *Allotment Architecture* (2013)
Andrea Brady: *Cut From the Rushes* (2013)

Narrative series

Ken Edwards: *Futures* (1998, reprinted 2010)
John Hall: *Apricot Pages* (2005)
David Miller: *The Dorothy and Benno Stories* (2005)
Douglas Oliver: *Whisper 'Louise'* (2005)
Paul Griffiths: *let me tell you* (2008)
John Gilmore: *Head of a Man* (2011)
Richard Makin: *Dwelling* (2011)
Leopold Haas: *The Raft* (2011)
Johan de Wit: *Gero Nimo* (2011)
David Miller (ed.): *The Alchemist's Mind* (2012)
Sean Pemberton: *White* (2012)
Ken Edwards: *Down With Beauty* (2013)
Philip Terry: *tapestry* (2013)

For updates on titles in print, a listing of out-of-print titles, and to order Reality Street books, please go to www.realitystreet.co.uk. *For any other enquiries, email* info@realitystreet.co.uk *or write to the address on the reverse of the title page.*

REALITY STREET depends for its continuing existence on the Reality Street Supporters scheme. For details of how to become a Reality Street Supporter, or to be put on the mailing list for news of forthcoming publications, write to the address on the reverse of the title page, or email **info@realitystreet.co.uk**

Visit our website at: **www.realitystreet.co.uk/supporter-scheme.php**

Reality Street Supporters who have sponsored this book:

Tim Allen
Bruce Andrews
Joanne Ashcroft
Alan Baker
Peter Bamfield
Tina Bass
Fred Beake
Chris Beckett
Charles Bernstein
John Bloomberg-Rissman
Philipp Blume
Andrew Brewerton
Jasper Brinton
Peter Brown
Clive Bush
Mark Callan
Duncan Campbell
John Cayley
Cris Cheek
Adrian Clarke
Stephen Clews
Norma Cole
Kelvin Corcoran
Claire Crowther
Marc V de Chantilly
David Dowker
Laurie Duggan
Carrie Etter
Gareth Farmer
Allen Fisher/Spanner
Timothy Freeborn
Jim Goar & Sang-yeon Lee
John Goodby
Giles Goodland
Paul Griffiths
Chris Gutkind

Charles Hadfield
Catherine Hales
John Hall
Robert Hampson
Randolph Healy
Colin Herd
Jeff Hilson
Peter Hodgkiss
Gad Hollander
Rob Holloway
Peter Hughes
Romana Huk
Michael Hunt
Elizabeth James &
Harry Gilonis
Keith Jebb
Mark Johnson
Nicholas Johnson
Pierre Joris
Trevor Joyce
L Kiew
Joshua Kotin
Bill Lancaster
Peter Larkin
Tom Leonard
Chris Lord
Antony Mair
Michael Mann
Peter Manson
Brian Marley
JCC Mays
Ian Mcewen
Laura McIntosh
Ian McMillan
Fabian McPherson
Peter Middleton

Richard Owens
Maggie O'Sullivan
Richard Parker
Gabrielle Perril
Dennis Phillips
Malcolm Phillips
Tom Quale
Peter Quartermain
Tom Raworth
Josh Robinson
Lou Rowan
Will Rowe
Anthony Rudolf
Barry Schwabsky
Gavin Selerie
Robert Sheppard
Iain Sinclair
Jason Skeet
Linus Slug
Pete Smith & Lyn Richards
Valerie & Geoffrey Soar
Jonathan Spratley
Andrew Taylor
Alan Teder
Michael Tencer
Philip Terry
Keith Tuma
Lawrence Upton
Robert Vas Dias
Juha Virtanen
Stephen Want
Sam Ward
John Wilkinson
Stephen Willey
Anonymous x 5

CPSIA information can be obtained at www.ICGtesting.com
Printed in the USA
LVOW11s1616301114

416286LV00004B/590/P

9 781874 400653